DATE DUE

9078

248.8
D'Av   D'Avila-Latourrette, Vict
         A monastic year

DATE DUE	BORROWER'S NAME	ROOM NUMBER
JE 11 '97	D. MARTEN	

248.8   9078
D'Av   D'Avila-Latourrette, Vict
         A monastic year

A Monastic Year

Also by Brother Victor-Antoine d'Avila-Latourrette

A Monastic Year

Reflections from a Monastery

Brother Victor-Antoine d'Avila-Latourrette

Taylor Publishing Company
Dallas, Texas

Copyright © 1996 Brother Victor-Antoine d'Avila-Latourrette

Published by Taylor Publishing Company
1550 West Mockingbird Lane
Dallas, Texas 75235

Library of Congress Cataloging-in-Publication Data
D'Avila-Latourrette, Victor-Antoine.
    A monastic year : reflections from a monastery / Victor-Antoine
d'Avila-Latourrette.
        p.   cm.
    Includes bibliographical references and index.
    ISBN 0-87833-923-X
    1. Monastic and religious life.   I. Title.
    BX2435.D33   1996   96-24019
    248.8'942—dc20   CIP
Printed in the United States of America

10   9   8   7   6   5   4   3   2   1

+

PAX

To François Letaconnoux and his family,

whose heartfelt love for St. Benedict and the monastic tradition

has been manifested in manifold ways,

in particular through their affection and solicitude

for the monastery of

Our Lady of the Resurrection.

TABLE OF CONTENTS

Spring
The Sources of Monastic Life

Summer
Aspects of Monastic Life

Autumn
Work in Monastic Life

Foreword

That in all things God may be glorified.
RULE OF ST. BENEDICT

Monastic houses have served in unique ways for civilizations of the East and West for more than two millennia. Because we live in somewhat apocalyptic times, the Monastic Word and the Monastic Image become crucially important today. The Monastic Image is the image of a simple life lived in the midst of complexity. It is the image of joyful frugality, the perception of a rhythm of work and contemplation that intersects with all the rhythms of the seasons—the seasons of nature, church, and the heart. The Monastic Word is the sound of silence, the sound of being with God in the midst of clamor. It is the practice of inward prayer intersecting with the spoken word in all the settings of human work, play, and praise.

In theory, everyone should be able to organize a life of simplicity and centeredness wherever they are. In practice, it is not so. And so it is that being able to turn to monastic centers, where the Word and the Image come together in a life patterned by the hours of Divine Office, in days structured by silence, becomes the means of renewal for many who wish for centered lives, but whose living conditions work against that centeredness.

I have found this to be profoundly true in my own life. The days of retreat at Our Lady of the Resurrection Monastery—where the shining golden thread of the Benedictine Hours of Office, spoken and sung, bind together the times of deep silence, Lectio Divina, and simple chores—are healing days. I do not view monasticism as a retreat from the world but as an entry into its beating heart. Time spent in monastic retreat puts one in tune with that heartbeat and enables one to work in the world in rhythm with creation's most basic motions.

I am a scholar. There was a time, some centuries ago, when the university—the *universitas*—provided such grounding for the mind and spirit, but it no longer does. It is important, then, to identify, affirm, and support the grounding centers that are still to be found in our midst, the monastic houses, so they can continue the work that will not otherwise be accomplished. The monastic house not only nourishes the intellectual, it also nourishes the activists, the artists and craftspeople, and the ordinary hard-working human beings whose activities carry humanity from one day to the next. This nourishment makes us all more creative and less driven as we deal with problems of twentieth-century life. We may not think of monasteries as centers of social change, but in liberating people from more immediate pressures monasteries have indeed, both historically and in the present, provided society with some of the greatest shapers of new social forms. Monasticism is the womb of the future.

ELISE BOULDING
Professor of Sociology, Emeritus
Dartmouth College

Introduction

A man who stays in his place in life will not be troubled.
ABBA POEMEN, DESERT FATHER

According to monastic tradition, there are diverse ways of living the monastic life. A monk may live alone in the seclusion of a hermitage, live with two or three other monks in a skete (small monastery), or live in a monastery with a larger community. The monastic tradition also recognizes pilgrim itinerant monks, whose vocation is expressed through the ancient Christian practice of pilgrimage. Often without a permanent home, the pilgrim monk finds his vocation unfolding in the wide roads and narrow paths of God's big world. Individual monks may live out the mystery of their vocation in diverse geographical places; some may be called to dwell in a real physical desert, others to the quiet of the countryside or in the obscure anonymity of a city— in the midst of a noisy crowd. What matters to the monk is not so much how his life unfolds, but that he finds the place where God wants him to be. Then, as the wise Abba Poeman points out, he stays there. By putting concrete footings in a particular place, the monk can engage his whole being in the all-consuming adventure of seeking God, which is the one and only purpose for all monastic life.

Like St. Benedict, who said that he wrote his little *Rule* for beginners, I conceived this book as a small, simple, and modest introduction for beginners to the mystery of monastic life. In no way does it seek to compete with the wonderful and authoritative works on the subject by renowned scholars, whose books are found abundantly in monastic libraries. Throughout the years, I realized that among the people we receive in our small monastery there has been great interest in learning more about monastic life. Our visitors readily concede that they know little about this way of life or its origins. It is for people like this that I wrote *A Monastic Year*.

This book is also the result of a certain monastic experience. Here at Our Lady of the Resurrection, we are guided by St. Benedict's *Rule* as well as the early monastic tradition of both the Christian East and Christian West (especially the French tradition). Many monks and nuns relate their experience from St. Benedict's time forward to later monastic developments of the Middle Ages and nineteenth century. My experience has been to take the original intuition of St. Benedict and, through him, return instead to the original sources of monasticism—to the desert. I have found this ancient desert monasticism to be a direct link to the Gospel and an authentic expression of Jesus' teachings. The early monastic ethos of the desert was nothing but a real and explicit attempt to be a mirror of the Gospel. Primitive monasticism never sought to distinguish itself from other contemporary forms of Christian life; its only purpose was to take the Gospel literally and put it into practice.

During the turbulent third and fourth centuries, when the monastic movement was developing, the church community at the same time had been accepted and assimilated in the Roman Empire. Christianity then became the religion of the state, and, unfortunately, this meant that the Church had to compromise certain Gospel values in order to fit its new status comfortably. This arrangement was unacceptable to some early Christians. For them the solution was to withdraw to the desert, where they would try to live the truth of the Gospel without blemish, without compromise. This was not an easy task for the early monks and nuns, but they accepted the challenge, counting on the grace and power of the Spirit of God as the only aid in their strife. The same is true today: monks and nuns in their spiritual poverty have no other help but the Spirit of God as they pursue the monastic path in the footsteps of the Gospel. At Our Lady of the Resurrection, monastic life is simple and precarious, poor and insecure—as was that of the desert monks and nuns—but also brings inner peace, joy, and serenity, which are the direct fruits of holding on to the truth of the Gospels. The pages in this book hope to attest only to this.

Although *A Monastic Year* is about a single subject, its form (like life) is a bit eclectic. It follows the monastic year with the theme of seasons, for they play such a prominent role in the monk's daily life. His prayer and work are greatly shaped by them. As the book unfolds, each of the seasons unites with a monastic theme. "Winter" considers the rhythms of monastic life, the unique interaction of nature and the liturgical season. Much, therefore, concerns Advent, Christmas, and Epiphany—along with wintry episodes at the monastery and celebrations of monastic saints that fall within that time. "Spring" considers the sources of monastic life, its origins and tradition. It also explains how Lent, Easter, and Pentecost are lived in the monastery and their spiritual impact for the monk. "Summer" explores different aspects of monastic life, such as faith, obedience, humility, silence, and simplicity, and how all of us—monks and non-monks—can benefit from the inspiration and practice of such monastic values. "Autumn," as a crowning point, examines the theme of work in monastic life in all its dimensions: the work of love, the work of prayer, the work of God, the work of our hands, and more. Often, the main activities of monastic life have been defined as *Ora et labora,* "prayer and work," yet it is over-looked that the Desert Fathers and Mothers taught that prayer itself is work, perhaps the most difficult and enterprising kind of work. The book concludes with appendices comprising an extensive glossary of monastic vocabulary and a selected bibli-ography—all further avenues of monastic exploration for the intrigued reader.

In conclusion, I would like to thank all those who helped and supported me in the production of this small work. First of all, to Holly McGuire, my editor at Taylor Publishing Company, who commissioned and guided me with great understanding, patience, and wisdom as we proceeded with the manuscript. To Howard Sandum, my agent, for suggesting this book. To Fr. Andrew Mark Quillen of Glastonbury Abbey for his friendship and encouragement, and for reading parts of this work in progress. And lastly, but not least, to Sr. Joan Regis Catherwood, R.S.H.M., for typing most of the manuscript, and to Jonathan Henry, for typing the rest. May the Lord bless them abundantly—and also the reader, who through these pages I hope will discover and taste "how good is the Lord" to all who search for him in the desert of the monastic life.

BROTHER VICTOR-ANTOINE D'AVILA-LATOURRETTE
May 16, 1996
Solemnity of the Ascension of the Lord

Winter

The Rhythms of Monastic Life

Advent

Long is our winter,
Dark is our night;
Come, set us free,
O Saving Light!
FIFTEENTH-CENTURY GERMAN HYMN

As we enter into the season of Advent, our winter days grow shorter, the air grows colder, and a quiet stillness settles on the physical world at large. All living things that must survive the winter out-of-doors draw deep into themselves. The trees retract their sap, the forest animals hibernate, and the living creatures that continue to move around in the cold, snow-covered world take care to conceal their food stores.

Just as nature retreats deep into itself during the winter months, so the Christian is invited to turn inward during the blessed time of Advent in preparation for the Lord's coming. This inner preparation, helped by prayer, silence, Bible readings, and good works, is essential if we are to celebrate in a worthy manner the solemn commemoration of the Lord's birth on Christmas Day and during the whole of the Christmas season.

Advent is a quiet, contemplative time of waiting for the Light that will come and shine on us on Christmas Day, rescuing us from the great darkness and hopelessness we experience in our daily lives. Advent, then, is a very special season of hope that links the coming of the promised Messiah in Jesus with the coming of Christ into our own hearts after a period of preparation, and with the coming of Christ again at the end of time. Like other seasons of the liturgical year, Advent commemorates something of the past in order to heighten our awareness

of the same mystery at work in our own present lives and to fill us with hope about the still-awaited future.

The Eastern Christian tradition sees the Advent season as a time of waiting for the light that will first shine forth at Christmas and reach its peak on Epiphany, the Feast of Lights. The beautiful Isaiah text is then proclaimed during Liturgy: "Rise up in splendor! Your light has come, the glory of the LORD shines upon you. . . . Upon you the Lord shines, and over you appears his glory" (Isaiah 60:1–2, NAB).

It is a lovely thing to see that in the northern hemisphere, Christ's birth coincides with the victory of light over darkness in the physical world. After the winter solstice, about December 22, daylight slowly begins to lengthen, filling us with a sense of expectancy and promise. Likewise, during our Advent journey, our longing intensifies for the true Light who will be revealed on Christmas Day, thenceforth dispelling the darkness from the innermost parts of our hearts. During the long Advent nights, the church of the East prays in one of its liturgical texts, "To those who are caught in the night straying into the works of darkness, grant, O Christ, your light and your blessings."

Because we feel ourselves caught in an abyss of fear and darkness, we become deeply aware of our basic instinctual need for light, for the light of truth that is Christ (John 14:6). As we arrive at the end of our Advent journey and enter into the mystery of Christ's birth, "we rejoice with great joy" for, as another Byzantine text proclaims, "Our Savior, the Daysprings from on high, has visited us, and we who were in darkness and shadows have found the truth!" On Christmas Day, the intense longing of our Advent prayer "Come, Lord Jesus" is fulfilled, our hope becomes a promise renewed, and our darkness is vanquished by the radiant splendor of God's light.

> Lord Jesus Christ,
> Son of God and son of Mary,
> You are the radiant start of morning.
> Come and deliver us from our fears
> And the darkness in our everyday lives.
> As the Church in earlier times
> Once cried for you, we cry again with one voice:
> Come, Lord Jesus, come!
> Look with mercy upon us
> Who await your coming,
> And make shine on us
> Your saving light.

The Advent Journey

Eternal God who made the stars,
Your people's everlasting light!
O Lord, Redeemer, save us all,
And hear your servants when they call.

You came with healing power to save
A world that languished, self-condemned:
The wounds of sin were wide and deep,
The cure for guilt was your free gift.

The evening time of life was near
For all the world, when you came forth,
A bridegroom from your nuptial bed
Within the Virgin's spotless womb.
    "Conditor Alme Siderum," Advent hymn for Vespers

As one travels into the rural landscape of New York's Dutchess County during the early days of winter, one may glimpse from a distance the contemplative monastery of Our Lady of the Resurrection. Perched on a hilltop and surrounded by silent wintry woods, our small, secluded monastery lies only a few miles away from Millbrook, the nearest village. The brilliant incomparable foliage of autumn has disappeared, and the trees stand stark and bare. One of the delights of early winter is to gaze upon the sunset through the elaborate patterns of branches that partition the pink sky like the elegant tracery of a stained glass window. The trees, with their bare branches reaching quietly toward the light, seem to share in the pleading of our Advent prayer: "Come, Lord Jesus, Come."

Early Christians traditionally prayed with their arms outstretched toward heaven, from where the Lord was to come again. The winter trees with their branches outstretched is a symbolic reminder to me that the monk, too, especially during his Advent journey, must look at all times toward God in unceasing prayer and reach his open arms toward Him with deep desire.

Here in upstate New York, the weather is habitually sharp in early December, sometimes even fiercely cold. Snow may not yet cover the ground, but there is no doubt among us that it is winter. The arrival of the cold in our midst coincides with the arrival of Advent in the monastery.

For us monks, who see ourselves on a pilgrimage throughout life, the Advent season intensifies and deepens the sense of journey. The monastic journey moves forward with expectation toward an arrival, an encounter. The monk, secluded in his monastic solitude, longs and prays expectantly for the blessed coming of the Savior, the Lord Jesus Christ.

In the monastery there is something special about Advent, and something of it is felt immediately the moment the Vespers hymn, "Conditor Alme Siderum," is intoned in the choir. Through the lilting Gregorian melody, one senses the deep inner joy that comes with the season. From the years of singing time and again the same melodies of the monastic chant for each particular feast or season, they have grown into us, giving the awareness of how beautifully they express the rich meaning of the season. The Gregorian chant, sanctified by centuries of monastic use, has its own unique way of conveying something of the mystery commemorated in our liturgical prayer. We must never forget the fact that the chant is not music or melody alone, but it is words *and* music, and the music was written to fit the words, not the other way around, thus making the chant truly a vehicle of prayer. The Gregorian Advent melodies, with their simplicity and serene beauty, have a way of transforming our vocal sounds into acts of praise and adoration to our eternal God, for all his wonderful deeds among us.

Among the antiphons of Vespers for the First Week of Advent, there is one in particular that nurtures in me the Advent message of hope and reflects the loveliness of the season: "*In illa die stillabunt montes dulcedinem . . .*" "On that day [of the Lord's coming] sweet wine will flow from the mountains, milk and honey from the hills, alleluia."

> Advent is primarily about the coming of God, and only in a secondary way about our asking, seeking, waiting, and longing. There is hope, because we are unconditionally loved, whatever may be our failures, our tepidity, or our secret despair. The word "Come" is a bearer of mystery.
>
> MARIA BOULDING, *The Coming of God*

St. Nicholas

O Holy Father Nicholas,
The fruit of your good deeds has enlightened
And delighted the hearts of the faithful.
Who cannot admire your measureless patience and humility?
And who cannot wonder at your graciousness to the poor?
At your compassion for the afflicted?
O Bishop Nicholas,
You have divinely taught all things well.
And now wearing your unfading crown,
You intercede for our souls with Christ, our God.
Byzantine Vespers of St. Nicholas

At the outset of Advent, a season that speaks to us deeply of hope because "the Lord is near," as the Liturgy announces, we celebrate the feast of St. Nicholas (December 6). His feast is an important pause on our Advent journey, for his life is an example of Gospel living for Christians of all times and places.

Among the many icons of saints that fill our humble monastic chapel with a certain mysterious presence, the icon of St. Nicholas stands out vividly. Because my place in the chapel is almost right in front of this icon, I have occasion several times a day to gaze on it while I am at prayer. What is particularly striking about this icon is the fact that the saint is not represented alone. St. Nicholas is in the center with arms outstretched, but all around him, as a kind of frame to his presence, are episodes of the many good deeds he performed and the many people he helped during his lifetime.

I can't help but think how appropriate it is for Christians today to reflect on the humble example of St. Nicholas. His life, a rather ordinary one, was given entirely to prayer and good works. He was not a monk, writer, or teacher, but he preached daily to his people the Word of God and lived by it. He battled for the rights of the poor and oppressed and vigorously defended the rights of widows and orphans. We would say today that St. Nicholas was a saint with a social conscience. I prefer to think he was a saint with a Gospel conscience.

Like Jesus, his Lord and Master, St. Nicholas was a good shepherd to his flock, exercising special compassion and mercy toward the outcasts, the poor, the undesirables of his time, and all those who were in distress in one form or another. His gentle goodness and exemplary life radiated beyond the boundaries of his own diocese of Myra, attracting many unbelievers to faith in Jesus, the Messiah.

The life of St. Nicholas holds great value for our time, not just as we prepare ourselves for Christmas, but as our entire lives unfold under a societal climate not unlike that of the time of St. Nicholas. His example and preaching, in total consonance with the Gospel, is the antithesis of the rhetoric of meanness and self-centeredness preached by many politicians today: that the poor, the elderly, and immigrants are enemies for whom compassion is too costly. In such times, intolerance of those who appear different from the social norm because of race, language, nationality, or sexual orientation is countenanced. It saddens me deeply that some who sponsor such policies call themselves Christians, when these ideas are in direct opposition to the Gospel of Jesus. All we have to do is read Matthew 25:31–46 to be reminded where the Gospel stands on these matters. And what an irony, that these same people would like into introduce prayer in the schools as a way of honoring God, thus showing they are "good Christians"! To them, I would quote what the Lord himself harshly says in Matthew 15:7–9: "Hypocrites! It was you Isaiah meant when he so rightly prophesied:

This people honors me only with lip service,
while their hearts are far from me.
The worship they offer me is worthless."

Political parties or labels don't mean very much to me, as a
Christian monk, one way or another. It is part of the world one
leaves behind in order to follow Jesus. But though politics
do not mean much to me, policies do, as they should to all
Christians. Policies usually either promote or are opposed to
Gospel values. It is our duty not only to pray but even to speak
out when need be for the sake of the Gospel. In a chaotic and
selfish world, where greed, hatred, intolerance, punishment,
revenge, and discrimination become the exalted values of a
society, the Christian, like St. Nicholas, must gently but firmly
proclaim the love and selflessness of Jesus, the peace, compassion, and mercy of the Gospel. We must look at the present
political and cultural climate in this country and the whole
world, as Nicholas, the humble disciple of the Lord, would:
as a challenge from God to take the Gospel seriously and to
proclaim it with our very lives. This is the grace we must pray
to God for on St. Nicholas's lovely feast day.

Merciful God,
In your love for us, your children,
You inspired St. Nicholas
To deeds of kindness and compassion for the poor.
Help us, after his example,
To serve the poor, the hungry,
The dispossessed, and the lonely
In the true spirit of the Gospel.
Give us the grace
To walk in the footsteps of the Gospel
Without fear,
And to proclaim it with joy
All the days of our lives.

The Advent Wreath

Holly and Ivy, Box and Bay
Put in the church on Christmas Day.
FIFTEENTH-CENTURY ENGLISH CAROL

Our small monastery chapel is quite austere (as it should be!), especially during Advent and Lent, when there are no flowers or decorations in it. The only exception is the Advent wreath. In fact, we usually have two Advent wreaths each year, one in the chapel and one at the table in the refectory. These are the only green decorations throughout the monastery before Christmas Day itself.

The custom of the Advent wreath—with its four candles, three purple and one pink—originated in antiquity in the Germanic countries and was passed on from paganism to Christianity. Burning lights and fires during the darkest month (December, or Yule, as it was called then) was part of the folk celebrations enthusiastically anticipated by northern Europeans each year. In the early sixteenth century during the days of Reformation, some Christians conceived the idea of introducing this ancient custom, with its symbolism of lights, into their Advent practices, changing it from a pagan custom into a Christian one, Christ being, of course, both the symbol of Light and the Light of the World. In Germany the custom took hold among both Protestants and Catholics, was introduced to monasteries of the surrounding region, and spread from there to the rest of the world.

Here in the monastery, we eagerly await both the preparation of the wreath, usually made of fresh evergreen boughs found on the property, and then the lighting of the first candle

on the first Sunday of Advent. In following evenings, before sitting down to supper, we light the candle of that particular week, sing an Advent hymn, and recite the appropriate prayer.

The lighting of the candle provides a moment of intense joy and anticipation, for the candle's peaceful light announces the approaching celebration of the Lord's birth. After the prayer, as we sit to eat, all other lights are put out, and the radiant light from the Advent wreath, with its cheerful and gentle glow, comforts us in an intimate way. It is indeed a very rich moment in the monastic day, a moment filled with promise, peace, prayer, longing, and joyful expectation, for the birth of the Savior is at hand. The cry of the early Church resounds again and again in the heart of the monk: Come, come, Lord Jesus. Come O Thou, the fulfillment of a promise!

> In darkness there is no choice.
> It is light that enables us to see
> the differences between things:
> and it is Christ who gives us light.
>   C. T. WHITMELL

Johann Sebastian Bach: Minstrel of God

Savior of the nations come,
Virgin's son, make here Thy home!
Marvel now, O heaven and earth,
That the Lord chose such a birth.

Not by human flesh and blood,
By the Spirit of our God,
Was the Word of God made of flesh,
Woman's Offspring, pure and fresh.

Wondrous birth! O Wondrous Child
Of the Virgin undefiled!
Though by all the world disowned,
Still to be in heav'n enthroned.
> JOHANN SEBASTIAN BACH CHORALE,
> "NUN KOMM, DER HEIDEN HEILAND"

The season of Advent provides us with diverse sources of spiritual food and joy. Among those which I find to be of great help, enhancing my inner journey toward Christmas, are the Advent cantatas of Johann Sebastian Bach. One of Bach's greatest gifts, perhaps not always well known, is that much of his music is principally inspired by faith and thus expresses a profound theology. It is not a surprise, therefore, that some throughout history have called him the Fifth Evangelist.

The inspiration for Bach's music—especially religious music like the cantatas, the Masses, and the Passions—came from his deep, intimate devotion to Christ, his Lord and Savior.

This devotion to the Lord was totally consistent with the personal piety encouraged by the Lutheran church of Bach's time. Although admiring Bach's prodigious creativity and enjoying his music immensely, music lovers often are ignorant of the spiritual inspiration of his music. Bach was a wondrous musician, but he was above all a man of faith, and it was this faith that motivated his great compositions. His music was a vehicle to express the Christian faith that nurtured him and to which he adhered all of his life. Just as religious icons are often referred to as "theology in colors," one could describe Bach's compositions as "theology in music," for it is faith that forms the bedrock of his music. At the beginning of each of his compositions, Bach usually inscribed the letters *SDG:* "Soli Dei Gloria," "to God alone the Glory." He was always careful to express his personal faith in his music and texts. Bach did not experience a conflict between secular and sacred music, which is often the case with contemporary composers. His faith was totally practical, bringing all aspects of life together and centering them in God, the one source of all good inspiration.

Bach, like many other pious Christians of his time, loved the Bible. Albert Schweitzer, who studied the notations in Bach's personal Bible, described him as "a Christian who lived with the Bible." In a notation about 2 Chronicles 5:13, Bach wrote, "N.B. At reverent performance of music, God is always at hand with his gracious presence."

The Advent cantatas, which I usually listen to in the morning while doing manual work, have become a part of my regular Advent practice throughout the years. These cantatas were primarily written in Leipzig during the many years that Bach was choirmaster of the Church of St. Thomas, where today he lies buried. As I listen to these cantatas again and again, year after year, they have become a source of spiritual blessing and an inspiration to prayer. Listening to them, one feels immediately drawn to a contemplative, prayerful spirit, a spirit appropriate at all times for a monk, but in particular during the days of Advent. The expectation expressed in the Advent cantatas finds its fulfillment in Bach's *Christmas Oratorio,* which is *de rigeur* during the Christmas octave here and in many other monasteries around the world.

J. S. Bach has been called "God's greatest musical servant since King David," for what David has done with the Psalms, Bach has also accomplished with his music. Bach lived and died faithfully, adhering to the end to the one principle that inspired all of his life: "The aim and fundamental reason of all music is none other than to be the Glory of God and the recreation of the human spirit."

> Praise God in his holy place,
> Praise him in his mighty heavens.
> Praise him for his powerful deeds,
> Praise his surpassing greatness.
>
> O praise him with sound of trumpet,
> Praise him with lute and harp.
> Praise him with timbrel and dance,
> Praise him with strings and pipes.
>
> O praise him with resounding cymbals,
> Praise him with clashing of cymbals.
> Let everything that lives and that breathes
> Give praise to the Lord. Alleluia!
> PSALM 150, PSALTER, GRAIL VERSION

The O Antiphons

O wisdom from the Father's mouth,
The Word of his eternal love,
Beneath whose firm yet gentle sway
This world is governed from above.
O come! O come!
And teach us all
The ways that lead to life.
       MAGNIFICAT ANTIPHON FOR DECEMBER 17

Beginning December 17, our sense of Advent expectation inten-
sifying, our longing for the Redeemer finds perfect expression in
the so-called O Antiphons, which are solemnly sung each
evening at Vespers in all monasteries until December 23. These
seven antiphons are known as the O Antiphons, because each
starts with the vocative O: "O Wisdom," "O Adonai," "O Root
of Jesse," "O Key of David," "O Daystar," "O King of All
People," "O Emmanuel."

    The O Antiphons, written and sung in the second
Gregorian mode of the chant, were all composed according to
the same formula in the original Latin. Each begins with an
invocation to the Lord that expresses his attributes or messianic
titles, then culminates with a longing call and prayer or concrete
petition: "O come! and set us free, delay no longer in your
love." The exquisite Gregorian melody, which is the same for
the seven O Antiphons, expresses beautifully the meaning of the
texts, with all of their rich complexity and movement.

    The arrival of the beautiful O Antiphons is enthusiasti-
cally awaited each Advent in every monastery and sung with the
utmost reverence and solemnity. Usually the antiphon is first

9078

intoned by the abbot or superior of the monastery, who is
attended by two monks bearing candles as in the most solemn
occasions. Then all the monks join in, while the altar is incensed
and the monastery bells ring in sounds of joy and praise during
the antiphon and the Magnificat. It is the highlight of the
evening liturgical prayer of Vespers, and those who experience it
even once never forget it.

A few years ago, while doing some research into the
origins of these ancient antiphons in the monastic Office, I
found that they were already known in Rome in the second half
of the sixth century, during the time that Advent was being
elaborated there as a liturgical season. However, it could well
be that these antiphons date to an even earlier time, that of the
Gallican Rite, such as it was practiced in the south of France and
northern Spain. For Advent as a liturgical season was indeed
created in France, then Gaul, within the Gallican Rite. There are
traces of these antiphons in a poem written in Gaul around
AD 750, and they are certainly found in the early antiphonary of
Saint Corneille de Compiegne, composed between AD 860 and
AD 880. The first manuscript in which one finds all of them
together and which remains in use to this day comes from the

ancient abbey of St. Gall in Switzerland, the manuscript dating back to the year 1000.

These beautiful, evocative antiphons, sung according to the purest lines of the Gregorian chant, create a particular climate of serenity and intense peace in the monk's heart during the last days of our Advent journey, just as Christmas approaches. This monastic climate of serenity opens wide the doors of the heart to the silence and joys of prayer and contemplation. In the depths of our hearts we know with certainty that Christ is coming. He is our Savior, and thus we long for him with inexpressible desire. As evening falls over the universe during the singing of Vespers and day gives place to the darkness of night, one is filled with hope and increased yearning for the arrival of the Light that will shine on Christmas Day.

> O Daystar of unending light,
> The Sun of God's pure holiness,
> The splendor of the Father's face,
> And image of His graciousness.
> O come! O come!
> And lead us forth from darkness
> And the gloom of death.
> O ANTIPHON FOR DECEMBER 21

CHRISTMAS

In Bethlehem in a manger of dumb beasts,
From a virgin now is born a young child
Who is the pre-eternal God.
O what a wonder is this!
BYZANTINE MATINS OF THE FOREFEAST OF THE NATIVITY

This simple, short text from the Byzantine Office expresses to us concretely the mystery we celebrate on Christmas Day and throughout the length of this particular liturgical season. First of all, the text is an affirmation, without a trace of a doubt, of the fact of the Incarnation. For the "young child" is also "the pre-eternal God," and He is "from a virgin now born." Mary gave flesh to the Word, and so Christmas in a unique way is also a feast of the Mother of God.

The text also tells us that Jesus, the Son of God and son of Mary, is born "in Bethlehem" in the company and "manger of dumb beasts." In those days, Bethlehem was a small, forsaken village, despised by the great of the world. Thus, from the very beginning of his appearance into this world, Jesus, the Son of the Most High, embraces a state of lowliness and casts his lot among the poor, the destitute, the forgotten and undesirables of this world. The first ones to receive the good news of the birth of the Savior were the humble, poor shepherds of the surrounding region, who were taking "turns to watch their flock during the night" (Luke 2:8). To them the angel of the Lord said, "Do not be afraid. Listen, I bring you news of great joy, a joy to be shared by the whole people. Today in the town of David a savior has been born to you; he is Christ the Lord. And here is a sign for you: you will find a baby wrapped in swaddling clothes

and lying in a manger" (Luke 2:10–12). Thus, the humble shepherds and the dumb beasts were among the first, together with Mary and Joseph, to offer homage and adoration to the little child lying in the manger, their Lord and God. "O what a wonder is this." And what a lesson it contains for us all! From the moment of his birth to the moment of his death, Jesus deliberately and clearly shows us where his preference lies and the way that we his disciples must follow.

As we celebrate once more this beautiful feast of the Incarnation, let us pray for the grace to learn the admirable lessons the Lord wishes to teach us through the example of his holy birth. May Our Lady, St. Joseph, and the humble shepherds inspire in us the courage to follow the Lord Jesus faithfully in his self-emptying and in his preference for the poor and lowly, even though it may be today as it was then, so contrary to the values of the world.

> Today Christ is born!
> Today the Savior has appeared.
> Today the angels sing on earth,
> And the archangels rejoice.
> Today the just exult, saying:
> Glory to the Lord in the highest. Alleluia.
> MAGNIFICAT ANTIPHON FOR CHRISTMAS DAY

Solemnity of
the Mother of God

Holy Mother of God, save us.
Byzantine prayer

In the very first Christian centuries, the early Christians
honored Mary, the mother of Jesus. The Gospels describe the
highly eminent role assigned to Mary in the unfolding mystery
of our salvation. Mary is present from the very beginning, from
the moment of the conception and birth of the Savior, and she is
also present at the end, at the foot of the Cross.

Among all the titles ascribed to Mary throughout the ages,
the most significant one was given to her by the early Christian
Church, united in solemn council at Ephesus in 431. There,
moved by the Holy Spirit, the Church of God proclaimed her to
be the *Theotokos,* the "God-bearer," that is to say, the Mother of
God. The Mother of God is proclaimed to be an integral part of
the mystery of Jesus Christ, the mystery that was in God's mind
before the ages began.

The mystery of the Mother of God, embedded within the
depths of the mystery of Christ Himself, is therefore very dear
and very sacred to the Christian faithful but ever beyond their
comprehension. In most icons of the Mother of God, she is
portrayed carrying the Christ Child in her arms. There we see
that while the eyes of Jesus rest lovingly upon His mother, her
gaze is directed tenderly toward us and toward all those who
approach Him. She shows her Son to each of us, silently saying,
"Behold your God and your Savior."

In the Gospels as in the icon, the Mother of God is always
portrayed in physical proximity to Jesus and is always pointing

to Him. In the Magnificat, her song of praise, she calls herself "God's lowly handmaid," showing us the depths of her self-effacing attitude before the immense mystery of Jesus Christ. She is only the humble creature who bore him, the Son of God. It is God alone who has done great things in her. It is therefore to him alone, Mary would tell us, that all our adoration, our praise, and our worship belong. It is to him alone that our obedience and the undivided attention of our hearts must be given.

As we are allowed to enter with the eyes of faith into the mystery of Christ, we rejoice with great joy as we discover that Mary is both the Mother of God and also our mother. She has engendered us at the foot of the Cross when Jesus said to her "Woman, this is your son" (John 19:26). As Jesus commits the beloved disciple John to the maternal care of His mother, so does He also entrust us to her. In the person of John, it is all of us who become children of Mary.

The presence of the Mother of God in our lives is then very real. She is our mother, our friend, our helper, our refuge in time of danger, and consolation in time of affliction. She is our luminous guide when we lie in darkness and in the midst of despair. On our journey toward God's kingdom, her warm presence dispels our sense of loneliness. She gives us the strength and courage needed for the journey. We walk, but never alone, for the Mother of God is always with us. If we remain quiet and don't interfere or fuss too much about ourselves, we should be able to feel her consoling presence as we pray the ancient prayer:

> We entrust ourselves to your protection,
> Holy Mother of God.
> Listen to our prayers,
> Help us in our daily needs,
> And save us from every danger,
> O glorious and blessed Virgin.
> *Sub Tuum Praesdium,* FOURTH-CENTURY PRAYER

A New Year

*Whatever a man may possess over and above what is
necessary for life, he is obliged to do good with, according
to the command of the Lord, who has bestowed on us the
things we possess.*

St. Basil the Great, *The Morals, I*

One of the first monastic feasts of the New Year is the feast of
"our holy father St. Basil" (January 2), as St. Benedict lovingly
calls him in the holy Rule, acknowledging him to be one of the
great fathers of monasticism. St. Benedict was forever grateful
to St. Basil and to all the earlier fathers and mothers of the
monastic tradition, which he in turn would amplify and expand
for new generations of monks and nuns in the West.

St. Basil the Great was born in Cappadocia around 330
and died there in 379. He was born into a remarkable old family
of wealth and distinction, in which the grandparents, the
parents, the brothers, and the sisters were all numbered among
the saints. He received a solid classical education in the schools
of Caesarea, Athens, and Constantinople, then settled in the
region of Pontus, where he consecrated himself wholeheartedly
to the communal form of monastic life. He had a vast influence
on the early development of the monastic movement, particularly in the East, where many monks and monasteries still
follow the general principles of monastic life he laid down for
his disciples. St. Basil was not only a great monk but also a great
bishop and father of the church, a charismatic man filled with
the Holy Spirit, whose writings and wisdom are still a source of
nourishment for our spiritual lives today, as they have always
been.

Upon entering the secular New Year and often hearing the expression "Happy New Year" being exchanged among friends and family members, the monk pauses to reflect upon the true meaning of a new year. Very often, when someone says, "Happy New Year," the greeting seems to convey the simple idea that we are adding one more stage to the expansion of our lives, and that one hopes it will be a good one from a material point of view. This attitude presents a very shallow picture of life as a succession of years. This is a rather sad and almost fatalistic way of looking at life and at the new year ahead of us.

Some of the greeting cards we receive in the mail speak also of happiness and prosperity for the New Year. While these good wishes are offered to us by friends with deep sincerity, the monk cannot help but reflect on how both happiness and prosperity are at times of a transient or elusive nature. For the monk, entering into a new year is serious business. It gives him the occasion to look deeply into the mystery of time, which in turn reminds him of his own mortality—the years are fleeting and indeed pass by quickly, in no time evaporating into the mystery of eternity. This is why the monk can't help but use the beginning of a new year to remind himself of those intangible realities that are essential for daily living and that no one can take away from us, such as peace, hope, and growth of love.

To be at peace with God, with oneself, and with all those one interacts and lives with is a more precious gift than all the wealth of the world assembled. To be anchored in hope—a hope that helps us accept without complaint both the blessings and the sufferings that are found in daily life, a hope that reveals to us each moment the presence of a loving God who is watching over us and standing by our side throughout all of life's circumstances—is a more comforting, fulfilling, and desirable thing than all the empty prosperity the world can offer.

As the New Year comes upon us, the monk, in his monastic solitude, prays to the Lord of the universe to grant everyone the gift of peace and the blessing of hope. The prayer does not end there; it continues throughout the rest of the year.

> No heaven can come to us unless our hearts
> find rest in today, Take Heaven!
> No peace lies in the future which is not hidden
> in this present instant. Take Peace!
> The gloom of the world is but a shadow.
> Behind it, yet within reach . . . is Joy.
> There is radiance and glory in the darkness, could we
> but see,
> And to see we have only to look;
> I beseech you to look.
> FRA GIOVANNI DI CAPISTRANO

The Days are Short, the Weather's Cold

Fireside happiness, to hours of ease
Blest with that charm, the certainty to please.
JOHN WILMOT, EARL OF ROCHESTER, FROM "HUMAN LIFE"

The winters here in upstate New York and New England are legendary for their intense cold and long duration. Our small monastery has three wood stoves to provide us some relief from the cold, and one daily duty during winter consists of tending the stoves at regular intervals. Part of our monastic day in wintertime is spent in vigorous outdoor work, either splitting and piling the wood or carrying it indoors for our daily supply. In our monastic enclosure, there is plenty of wood available for that specific purpose. I don't like to see our trees cut, but Providence in its own way sees that we often find fallen trees or others damaged beyond repair by a merciless storm. Very often, too, some of our trees are in such close proximity to each other that they are in dire need of thinning out. There are more than enough varieties of trees in this monastic land: birch, hickory, hemlock, maple, and many more. To them we are grateful for providing needed heat for the cold winter months.

At times the outdoor winter work may seem a bit too arduous; nevertheless, besides being a necessity, I find it to be challenging and invigorating. Since the garden has been put to rest for the season, the continuing care of the monastery animals and the wood work provides me enough outdoor activities to balance the daily monastic routine.

Filling and tending the monastery stoves provides me another one of those joys in which I delight heartily, the occasion to enjoy some quiet time. On certain days when the temperature is below zero, the monastic buildings are covered by inches and inches of snow, and fierce, gusty winds can be heard in the background, it is indeed a peaceful pleasure to spend time around the stoves, watching the fire rising straight upward in the chimneys, listening to its cracking sound in the deep silence, and of course being comforted by its warmth. I always find that parcel of time spent in the evening by the fireplace to be very restful and immensely soothing for the inner spirit. There is great tranquillity and a particular quality of soul delight during those quiet moments of prayer, reading, and utter silence.

The mysterious, complex reality that a fire embodies speaks volumes to me, sometimes concretely and sometimes abstractly. Fire has a way of insinuating something about the eternal verities in which the life of the monk is plunged. The Apostle Paul describes God as a consuming fire, a mystical image that readily resonates in the monastic heart. Fire, one of the most basic elements of nature, has its own vivid way of revealing, to those who wish to see, something undefinable about the presence of God.

> Praise be, my Lord, for Brother Fire,
> By whom Thou lightest up the night:
> He is beautiful, merry, robust, and strong.
>   St. Francis of Assisi, *Canticle of the Creatures*

Epiphany of the Lord

All you who seek the gentle Christ,
To heaven lift your eyes and see
The sign of glory without end,
Revealing his descent to earth.

This gleaming star outshines by far
The brightness of the sun's full glow,
For it declares that God made man
Has come to bless and save us all.

He is the king of nations all,
Expected by the Jews of old,
The promised seed of Abraham,
Born of his race in course of time.

All glory, Jesus, be to you,
Revealed to all the nations now,
To God the Father glory be
And to the Spirit endlessly. Amen.
    PRUDENTIUS, "QUICUMQUE CHRISTUM,"
    EPIPHANY HYMN FOR LAUDS

As we reach the beautiful feast of the Epiphany of the Lord, the joyful days of Christmastime in the monastery come to a close. In ancient times the feast was called Theophany, and it was celebrated on Christmas Day itself. In the fourth century, Pope Julius I made two different feast days out of the original one. Christmas remained fixed on December 25, and Epiphany was moved to January 6, twelve days afterward.

Epiphany means "manifestation," and in the Christian East the feast is still celebrated under its original name, *Theophany,* "manifestation of God." In the Latin Mediterranean countries, the feast was commonly known as *Festum Trium Regem,* "Feast of the Three Kings." In the English-speaking countries, it was known as the Twelfth Day of Christmas. Epiphany is also often referred to as the Feast of Lights, the name being taken from the beautiful passage from the prophet Isaiah (60:1–3, 19; NAB) read both during the Office of Matins and again later on at Mass:

> Rise up in splendor!
> Your light has come,
> The glory of the Lord shines upon you.
> See, darkness covers the earth,
> And thick clouds cover the peoples;
> But upon you the LORD shines,
> And over you appears his glory.
> Nations shall walk by your light,
> And kings by your shining radiance. . . .

No longer shall the sun
Be your light by day,
Nor the brightness of the moon
Shine upon you at night;
The LORD shall be your light forever,
Your God shall be your glory.

The feasts of Christmas and Epiphany celebrate the
mystery of the Incarnation of Christ, God made as man. And
Christ is the Light of the world, which is why the rich
symbolism of light, especially during our long, dark winter
days, is particularly cherished by all those who celebrate the
feasts. The last antiphon of the first Vespers of the solemnity,
very expressive in the Gregorian chant, proclaims, "This
wondrous star shines like a flame, and points out God, the King
of Kings. The Wise Men saw it and offered their gifts to the
great King."

There are many monastic customs varying from country
to country and from monastery to monastery, associated with
the feast of the Epiphany. One beautiful ancient custom that
remains alive to this day in almost all monasteries is the solemn
announcement during Mass of the dates for the movable feasts
of the coming year: Ash Wednesday, Easter, Ascension,
Pentecost, and, at the end, the first Sunday of Advent. The
announcement proclaims, "As we have recently rejoiced over
the birth of our Lord Jesus Christ, now through the mercy of
God, we can look forward to the happiness that will stem from
the Resurrection of the same Lord and Savior." With Epiphany
we in the monastery reach the peak of our Christmas celebrations. Then the year proceeds seemingly slowly, as winter
follows its normal course, and our monastic solitude becomes
more complete during the cold months. Not too far on
the horizon, however, is the arrival of the Lenten-spring, with
its hidden promise of Easter joy.

O Christ, a light transcendent
Shines in thy countenance
And none can tell the sweetness,
The beauty of thy grace.

In this may thy poor servants
Their joy eternal find;
Thou callest them, O rest them,
Thou Lover of mankind.
                    JOHN OF DAMASCUS

St. Antony the Great, Father of Monks

His face had an extraordinary gracefulness; this too was a gift from the Lord; in fact, if those who didn't know him wanted to single him out when he was among a group of monks, they went towards him without looking at the others, attracted almost as it were by his features. And yet he differed in no way from the others as regards height or build, but only for his perfection of virtue and his purity of spirit.

St. Athanasius, *Life of St. Antony*

During our long winter solitude, the feast of St. Antony arrives on January 17. This is appropriate because Antony—the first monk, the Father of Monks—was a hermit and a lover of the solitary life in the desert.

St. Antony lived in Egypt between 251 and 356. At age eighteen he heard in church the Gospel text "If you wish to be perfect, go and sell all that you have, give it to the poor, and then follow me" (Luke 18:22). Antony, touched by grace, was so moved the moment he heard those words that he instantly decided to leave everything behind and retire to an unapproachable place in the Egyptian wilderness. In the solitude of the desert, Antony strove to center his entire life on God alone. This he did by means of continual prayer, meditation on the Word of God, manual work, discipline, and ascetic practices. In his old age, he imparted wisdom to his disciples and encouraged them to remain faithful to God till the end of the monastic life they had chosen. The life of St. Antony was written by the great father of the church and champion of faith St. Athanasius, who knew Antony personally. This life had such influence in both the East and the West, contributing to the expansion of the monastic ideal in the early Christian centuries and inspiring generations of monks, that St. Antony is rightly called the Father of Monks.

In our modest monastic chapel, next to the wood stove, hangs an icon of St. Antony. On special feast days, a small oil lamp is lighted in front of the icon during the monastic Offices. There is a certain something in this icon that speaks to me of the transformation by grace of the man Antony into the monk St. Antony. His presence in our midst, filled with a quiet nobility and inner radiance, seems to convey the truth of his words: "I no longer fear God, but I love him. For love casts out fear" (St. Antony, Apothegm 32). This love of God, which the humble monk Antony attained to such heights and degrees, continues to be today the sole reason for a Christian monastic life.

Always breathe Christ and trust Him.
ST. ANTONY'S LAST ADMONITION TO HIS DISCIPLES

CANDLEMAS:
A FEAST OF LIGHTS

Adorn your bridal chamber, O Sion,
And receive Christ, the King.
Greet Mary, the gate of heaven, with loving salutation;
For she carries the King of glory, the new Light.
In the temple stands the Virgin,
Embracing in her arms the eternal Son
Begotten before the day-star.
The elder Simeon receives Him in his arms
And proclaims to the nations:
He is the Lord of life and death,
The Savior of the world.
                "ADORNA THALAMUN TUUM, SION," ANTIPHON
                SUNG DURING THE PROCESSION OF THE FEAST

Forty days after the solemn Christmas festival, on February 2, the churches of the East and West celebrate the beautiful Feast of the Presentation of the Lord in the Temple, thus completing the cycle that started with Advent and peaked with Christmas and the Epiphany. This ancient feast originated, as do many of our Western liturgical feasts, in the Christian East, where it was known by its Greek name, the *Hypapante,* or the "Meeting" or the "Encountering." According to Mosaic law, forty days after the birth of a male child, the mother had to present him in the Temple while also making a sacrificial offering of a lamb or two turtledoves. This sacrifice served as purification for the mother after the birthing (in the West this feast was sometimes called the Purification of Mary). Jewish custom also asserted that all first-born creatures, whether human or animal, were to be consecrated in a special way to God. Mary and Joseph were known for always being obedient to all the precepts of Jewish law. Thus, on the appointed day, they brought the infant Jesus to the Temple, where, according to the Gospel story, he is received, blessed, and embraced by the elder Simeon and the righteous prophetess Anna (Luke 2:22–38). They both recognize in the young babe the Savior promised by God long ago to Israel. As they meet him for the first time in the flesh, their joy, which cannot be contained, is expressed in songs of thanksgiving and praise. The significance of the encounter of the elder and the recently born, helpless infant is expressed, I find, in terms of great tenderness and beauty in the Byzantine texts for the Offices of the day:

> Simeon tells us: Whom doest thou bear in thine arms,
> That thou dost rejoice so greatly in the Temple?
> To whom dost thou cry and shout:
> Now I am set free, for I have seen my Savior?
> This is he who was born of a Virgin;
> This is he, the Word, God of God,
> Who for our sakes has taken flesh
> To save humankind. Let us worship him!
> OFFICE OF GREAT VESPERS

This lovely, deeply touching feast of the Lord, impregnated with mystery, humility, and tenderness, has been dearly loved by monks and nuns throughout the ages and celebrated in most monasteries with great solemnity. First of all, there is the procession with hymn, antiphons, and candles through the monastic cloister, as the monks proceed toward the church for Mass. Processions are important, frequent rituals in monasteries, where they enhance, with both dignity and recollection, the spirit of the monastic liturgical celebration. The drama and decorum of monks in procession is particularly appropriate, I think, for

today's feast. The procession becomes a sort of cortege where the monks, united with Mary and Joseph, accompany the Lord as he enters the Temple to be offered to his Father. As the monks walk slowly in procession, we carry in our hands lighted candles that have just been blessed at the beginning of the rite.

Today's feast is commonly known by its English name, Candlemas, for candles play an important role in the liturgy of the day. The theme of light—based on the evocative words of Simeon, who calls the Christ Child "a light to enlighten the nations"—permeates the entire Liturgy of the feast. Today the Christian church reaffirms the truth of Simeon's words that Jesus is the true light of the world by placing the blessed candle in our hands. Thus, we also symbolically receive Christ in our hands and arms as the blessed Simeon and Anna once did long ago.

The fact that candles have such a prominent and central place in today's Liturgy is particularly important, I think, for those who follow the monastic way, for candles are in general very expressive of the devotional life of monasteries: there are the four candles of the Advent wreath, the Christmas candle lit on Christmas day, and the Easter candle lit during the whole of

Paschaltime. Then there are the everyday candles used during the celebration of the Eucharist and the monastic Offices, the candle that accompanies the Eucharist taken to a sick monk in his cell, and the candles and oil lamps lit in front of our icons, which convey to the Lord, to His holy Mother, and to God's friends the saints our humble homage and the silent petition of our prayers. The dancing yet steady flames of the candles in our chapel speak to me of those intangible realities the monk seeks and at times dimly perceives during his long hours of prayer. The comforting, ethereal aura springing from their light affirms for the monk the reality of a mysterious presence, a presence that can be sensed only with the eyes of faith. Candles are, in a way, messengers of him who is both mystery and the Invisible One.

> God created the world, and he bestowed upon it night and day. We know the sequence of darkness and light. But Christ is the true Light. He came into the world to give us the light that we may believe . . . and He commanded that our light, as Christians, should shine before men.
>
> MOTHER THEKLA, *Expressions of Faith*

St. Scholastica, Mother of Nuns

Let the Christian people rejoice
in the glory of the gracious virgin, Scholastica;
But most of all, let the choir of virgins and nuns
be glad celebrating the feast of her who,
Pouring forth her tears, entreated the Lord;
And because she loved so much,
she obtained greater power from him.
MAGNIFICAT ANTIPHON OF THE FEAST

During the chilly days of mid-February, when winter at times
begins to give us a hint of the forthcoming spring, we celebrate
in the monastery the feast of the very quiet and monastic
St. Scholastica (February 10). I call her a quiet saint, for so little is
known about her, and the little we know has come to us only
indirectly through Pope Gregory the Great's biography of
St. Benedict, her famous brother. Though little is known about
her, the portrait that Pope Gregory gives is one of a very human
and charming saint who makes the work of love and prayer the
operative reasons for her life.

Like her twin brother, Benedict, at a young age Scholastica
received from God the call to monastic life. Following in the
footsteps of her saintly brother, she entered a monastery of nuns
near Monte Cassino where St. Benedict was the abbot of a
monastery of monks. Once a year she was permitted to have a
visit with her brother, and they used this occasion to speak not
only of family matters but, more importantly, to speak of God
and their spiritual lives.

During one of those family visits, a most delightful episode took place. Toward evening, after a few hours of visiting with his sister, St. Benedict was getting ready to return to his monastery; such was the rule. Scholastica, however, begged him fervently to remain with her. Amazed and bewildered, Benedict refused his sister's request, reminding her of their obedience to the Rule and monastic custom. When Scholastica saw that her petition was of no avail, she laid her head in her hands on the table and prayed with tears in her eyes. A violent storm immediately broke, pouring torrential rain and making Benedict's return to his monastery impossible. At this, Scholastica ceased her praying and, looking at her brother with a smile, said to him, "Go now, Brother. Return to your monastery and leave me alone, if you can." Benedict guessed what had occurred and, smiling, reproached his sister, "May God forgive you, my sister. What have you done?" To this Scholastica replied with her usual simplicity, "I begged you to stay, and you would not listen to me, so I made recourse to my Lord in prayer, and He heard me." Accepting the divine will, Benedict acceded to his sister's wishes and remained with her until the following morning, sharing with her the joys of heaven. Gregory, commenting on the episode, said of her, "Greater was her power before the Lord, because greater was her love." After this visit, brother and sister didn't see each other again, for Scholastica died three days later. She had a premonition of her death but did not wish to make her brother aware of it. Upon learning of her death, Benedict ordered his monks to bury her in the monastery tomb prepared for him. So it was done, acknowledging that neither life nor death could separate these two.

Just as St. Benedict is acknowledged to be the Father of Monks in the West, so we can also rightly call St. Scholastica the beloved Mother of Nuns. We know that from the onset of monasticism in the desert, there were intrepid women who left behind the allures of the world in order to follow Christ via the monastic way. They contributed greatly to the monastic movement from the start. We learn from the writer Palladius, for instance, that during the early years of the desert movement, there were already twelve monasteries of women in the area around Thebes in Egypt. From some of the early monastic literature comes to us the names of such prominent and courageous women as the two Melanies, Macrina, Alexandra, Thais, Syncletica, Euphrasia, Mary of Egypt, Euphrosine, Paula, and Eustochia, along with the many other early nuns who not only emulated their brother monks in fervor but in fact often surpassed them in higher and more virtuous lives. The early monks, although very much men of their times and thus limited, acknowledged the extraordinary quality of these women monastics. Some monks wrote down the lives of the women, such as Mary of Egypt, for the edification of monks to come. As some of these authors came to recognize, it was the monks who were in need of imitating the sanctity and zeal of the early nuns.

The monastic life for us [women] is not in essence a battle but a way of love and faith. . . . For only in so glad a love can we make our senses follow after the spirit; hence it may be that women, who love much and intensely, find the fulfillment in monastic life which they always sought and which now absorbs them wholly.

MOTHER MARIA, *Sceptum Regale*

Spring

The Sources of
Monastic Life

The Monk

The monk is one who is separated from all,
yet is united to all.
    Evagrius Ponticos, fourth-century monk, *Practikos*

I believe that it is the witness of the monk to the
eternal, to preach the tenderness of God, and to live it.
    Mother Maria, *Her Life in Letters*

The word *monk* comes from the Greek *monachos,* "alone." The term is applied to one who makes the choice to lead a life that is solitary, unified, integrated, pacified, and undivided in the quest for the Absolute. For the sake of God, the monk leaves the world, its allures, pleasures, and all those ties which have been part of his life until now. This is painful and hard; after all, monks and nuns have much the same feelings and sensibilities as their fellow human beings.

The difference is that they have heard a call in their hearts, an inviting call that tells them, "Come. I am the Way, the Truth, and the Life. Follow me." The person who decides to become a monk or nun and enter the solitude of a monastery or hermitage does it because he or she has heard this call, a call stronger than any other, a call to communion and fullness of life with God, a call that fulfills the deepest desires of the human heart.

He is toil. The monk toils at all he does. That is what a monk is.
    Abba John the Dwarf, *The Sayings of the Desert Fathers*

Monastic Life: A Mystery

*To come face to face with the mystery of a monastic
vocation and to grapple with it is a profound experience.
To live as a monk is a great gift, not given to many.*
THOMAS MERTON

Monastic life, like any life, remains essentially a mystery. God
calls everyone in this world to a particular form of life, and
monastic life is precisely a response to a call. The monk's call is
to leave everything behind, as Christ invites us to do in the
Gospel, and to set out to seek God in silence and solitude.
Throughout the ages, monastic life has in essence been the experience of the desert. From the early centuries of Christianity, the
Holy Spirit has led certain men and women to the wilderness,
where they could hear his voice and he could speak to their
hearts. In the desert the Lord invites the monk to compunction
and true repentance, to continual prayer and adoration, to

voluntary silence, to the humble work of conversion of heart, which ultimately leads to the transfiguration of the monk's being by the power of God's love.

Very often monastic life is understood neither by our secular society nor even by many of our fellow Christians. The emphasis on self-denial, seclusion, and an absolute dedication to prayer makes some think that monastic life is a negative form of life. Some people think that monks and nuns are odd people who fly away from the company of other human beings and from the responsibilities of the world for some unknown reason. The truth, however, is just the opposite. Monks and nuns, and those who from time to time have come to share their life in a monastery, know that prayer totally opens their hearts to God and to the needs of their fellow human beings. If they choose to follow the path of self-renunciation, it is simply that they have heard Christ's invitation to this particular calling. While they retire to the desert of the monastic life to pray continually, monks and nuns also take in their hearts the concerns of all humanity. Prayer vastly expands the dimensions of the human heart, making it capable of containing both God and the entire human family. Monastic prayer, when perfected by grace, leads the monk and the nun to recognize Christ's presence in every human being.

> We can expect to spend our whole lives as monks entering deeper and deeper into the mystery of our monastic vocation, which is our life hidden with Christ in God. If we are real monks, we are constantly redis- covering what it means to be a monk, and yet we never exhaust the full meaning of our vocation.
> THOMAS MERTON, *The Monastic Journey*

Monasticism:
A Gift from the East

Thus, there were in the desert monasteries, which were
so many temples filled with heavenly choirs of men who
spent their lives singing the psalms, reading the sacred
Scriptures, fasting, praying, seeking their consolation in
the hope of joys to come, working with their hands in
order to give alms, living all together in a perfect
charity and a union worthy of admiration. Thus, one
could see in these places as it were an altogether
different country, cut off from the rest of the world, and
the fortunate inhabitants of that country had no other
thought than to live in love and justice.

St. Athanasius, *Life of St. Antony*

St. Athanasius described the life led by the early monks in the
Egyptian deserts, but the real origins of the monastic life are in
the Gospels, in the teachings and example of Jesus himself, and
in the prophetic figure of John the Baptist, whose voice cried
out in the desert, "Prepare the way of the Lord!" The monastic
ideal took root in the early years of Christianity, and it has
always remained an integral part of the life of the Church. From
the very beginning, there were Christians who took to heart
Christ's invitation to leave all they possessed to follow Him.
Obviously, the times have constantly changed since Christ first
uttered his invitation, but there has never been any lack of those
who hear the call, recognize his voice in the depths of their
hearts, and feel irresistibly compelled to leave everything behind
to follow him.

Since the time of St. Antony, many have felt the call to that mysterious place called the desert, the "wasteland," always the symbol and reality of total renunciation, where one went to do battle with the forces of evil and to seek God alone with purity of heart. For all monks, those following either the cenobitic or the eremitical life (in a monastic community or as a recluse, respectively), the desert remains the ideal prototype of what monastic life is meant to be: a generous renunciation of evil and of all that is not God; a dying to selfishness, so that the true self may emerge; a burning desire and a living thirst for God; and total fidelity to the smallest commandments of the Gospel, so that their lives may be transformed by the power of God's love and transfigured into his likeness.

As the Church was, Christian monasticism was born in the East. This is an important fact to keep in mind as we try to understand monastic life and see its continuity to our time. From the very early days of the Christian Church, there were ascetics and virgins who, while living at home, dedicated themselves to a more rigorous form of Christianity by spending long hours in prayer, practicing fasting, and caring for the poor, the sick, orphans, and widows. In the third century, the first forms of organized monastic life begin to appear in Egypt. Attracted by the example of Antony, other Christians began to settle in the desert, eager to be instructed by him who had become by then their spiritual father. By the time of Antony's death, there were colonies of monks and nuns both in the desert land and also all along the Nile River, seeking after God in the footsteps of the humble Father of Monks.

As the number of monks and nuns increased in the desert, the need for a more organized form of monastic life became apparent. At times some of the desert ascetics went to extremes, becoming known for their excesses in penance and other forms of asceticism. As a consequence, they sometimes tended to lose control over the real purpose of their monastic lives.

Just when they were in need of restoring equilibrium, the Lord sent a humble soldier to Tabennisi, a desert village along the east bank of the Nile, with the express purpose of reorganizing monastic life in the desert. His conception was a communal form of eremitical life where the brethren could lead lives free from the anxieties and dangers found in the wilderness. The soldier, Pachomius, created the first desert monastery by building a wall around the cells or huts of the monks, protecting them from the world and also joining them to one another. An abbot presided over the community as its head and spiritual mentor, and the monks gathered together weekly for his instruction and for their Sunday worship. The disciples of Pachomius followed a common rule, wore the same habit, attended the same Offices, and partook of the same work and meals. The discipline and order established by Pachomius in his monasteries enabled the monks to follow a monastic rhythm of life freer from the concerns of self and more attuned to the work of God in their souls.

At the same time that Pachomius was establishing monasteries, his sister Mary was organizing a community of nuns that could live together in a monastery not far from that of the monks. From the earliest appearance of monastic life in the desert, the presence of women was felt in its midst. These courageous women ascetics emulated the monks in their fierce determination to follow Christ, and they often surpassed their brothers in their fidelity and fervor.

The austere monastic life of the monks and nuns in the Egyptian desert became so admired by their fellow Christians that by the late fourth and fifth centuries, it had spread to Palestine, Syria, Armenia, Persia, Cappadocia, Gaul, Spain, and Italy. Late in the fourth century, another prominent monastic figure appeared on the Christian horizon: Basil the Great, a Greek who was highly educated and held in high esteem by the emperors, the bishops, and the learned laity. His great contribution to the early monastic movement was to enrich the communal form of monastic life with a solid theological grounding. St. Basil provided his monastery with a form of legislation called the Longer and the Shorter Rules, which tempered some of the Egyptian monastic practices and thus invited moderately motivated Christians to embrace the monastic state. Basil saw the monastic community patterned after the example of the early Christians (such as described in Acts 4:32), as the only place in which the true Christian ideals could be realized. For St. Basil the communal life provided the monks with the opportunity to practice fraternal charity, fulfilling the Lord's commandment to love one another. St. Basil's Rule was seen as a synthesis of all that was best in the monastic tradition, and it had a great influence both in the East and in the West. A Latin translation of St. Basil's Rule, early on brought to the West, served as the guide for many monasteries. The monastic ideal also came to the West via three very important figures, St. Martin of Tours, St. John Cassian, and St. Augustine. They established monastic centers in the West which fostered both the communal life and the striving for perfection of the individual monk.

These three and St. Basil were the worthy predecessors of St. Benedict, the inheritor of the monastic tradition of both the East and the West. Greatly influenced by St. Basil's Rule, St. Benedict—founding his monastery at Monte Cassino, seventy-five miles southeast of Rome, in 529—would create in his own Rule the most effective monastic synthesis of Eastern and Western traditions, a synthesis which has been faithfully transmitted for fifteen centuries, to our own days.

St. Benedict conceived the communal monastic life as "a school in the Lord's service" where monks could work together to attain their salvation and sanctification. For St. Benedict, the monk enters a monastery solely "to seek God," and in the pursuit of this ideal, he is encouraged by the mutual support and example of the brethren who are there for the same purpose. St. Benedict showed a great deal of wisdom and common sense in his Rule, pragmatically adapting the Eastern monastic pattern to the needs, customs, and culture of the West. By doing so, he was able to strengthen the community of his monks and make of it a living icon of what the Church of Christ ought to be like. This model of a perfect Christian community was for St. Benedict a reality that had eternal implications.

> The resilience and adaptability of the desert ideal to different circumstances and different ways of life was in fact one of its chief virtues.
> Douglas Burton-Christie, *The Word in the Desert*

Following Christ

*Jesus said, "If you wish to be perfect, go and sell what
you own and give the money to the poor, and you will
have treasure in heaven; then come, follow me."*

Matthew 19:21

These words from the Gospel seized the heart of St. Antony, the
first monk, and transformed his life forever. Jesus makes the
same invitation today to follow Him into the desert of the
monastic life. The monk, touched by grace and seized by the
love of Christ, slowly turns away from the ways of the world
and wholeheartedly gives himself to following the Lord.

The monastic life, consecrated exclusively to following
Christ, is lived in a spirit of great simplicity, humility, and
poverty according to the Gospel. The monk wishes to follow
the poor Christ and live in solidarity with those who still reveal
him to us: the poor, the oppressed, and the underprivileged
people of the world. In his daily life, the monk has concrete
ways of living out this identification with the poor, as through
his humble manual work. His diet, which includes fasting and
abstinence from meat, he joyfully accepts for Christ's sake,
mindful that a great many people of the world are starving and
are often exploited because of the affluence and waste embraced
by society. When he can, he gives individual assistance to those
in need. The spirit of the Beatitudes remains always the ideal for
all monks.

For St. Benedict, obedience is one of the most important
ways by which the monk imitates and follows Christ. In
Hebrews 5:8–9 we learn that although Jesus "was Son, he
learned to obey through suffering; but having been made

perfect, he became for all who obey him the source of eternal salvation." For the love of Christ, the monk willingly accepts submission to the will of another human being—the abbot, according to *The Rule of St. Benedict*—sacrificing his own will and desires in order to imitate more completely the example of his Master and Lord. It is not the abbot alone, however, that the monk is encouraged to obey. St. Benedict goes a bit further, inviting the monks to obey one another, thus walking in the steps of Christ: "Obedience is a blessing to be shown by all, not only the abbot, but also to one another as brothers, since we know that it is by this way of obedience that we go to God" (*The Rule of St. Benedict,* chapter 71).

The monk hears the Lord's exhortation to lose his own life in order to gain it, and it is in the experience of this paradox that the monk mysteriously finds his ultimate fulfillment.

> The great ends of the monastic life can only be seen in the light of the mystery of Christ. Christ is the centre of monastic living. He is the source and its end. He is the way of the monk as well as his goal.
> THOMAS MERTON, *The Monastic Journey*

✝HE GOSPEL

See how the Lord in His love shows us the way of life. Clothed then with faith and the performance of good works, let us set out on this way with the Gospel for our guide, that we may deserve to see Him who has called us to his kingdom.

Rule of St. Benedict, PROLOGUE

Since the life of the monk consists primarily in the imitation of Christ, the serious reading of, listening to, and study of the Gospel become the most vital element of his monastic day. He seeks to shape his life by the teachings of Jesus, by trying to follow with integrity and great fidelity even the smallest precepts of the Gospel, which leads him to the full knowledge of the revelation of God in Jesus Christ. It allows the monk to grow deeper and deeper in the "living experience" of he who reveals himself to the humble, the poor, the lowly, to the little ones.

St. Benedict encourages the monk to walk in the steps of the Gospel—for him, the monastery is "a school in the Lord's service," where the monk or nun comes to learn to live according to the teachings of the Gospel. There is nothing more important for the monk, to the mind of St. Benedict, than learning to know Christ through his Word and then completely identifying with him. According to St. Benedict, the monk or nun must assiduously spend several hours a day in Lectio Divina, that is, in reading and meditating on the Sacred Scriptures, in particular, the Gospels. By fidelity to this practice, the monk brings his whole being, with all its powers and faculties, into a life-giving encounter with the revealed Word of God. There, illumined by the Holy Spirit, he is nourished by the knowledge of God.

The reading, study, and prayerful pondering of the Word of God is a joint action undertaken at the same time by both God and the monk: God speaks and the monk listens. This interaction is the work of the Holy Spirit.

> Practice fasting; then meditate on the Gospel and the other Scriptures, and if an alien thought arises within you, never look at it but always look upwards, and the Lord will come at once to your help.
>
> MACARIUS THE GREAT, A DESERT FATHER

The Monastic Tradition

Tradition is the instrument of a perfect koinonia,
communion, both in forms and in spirit, throughout the
centuries and across frontiers.

BISHOP ANTONIE PLOIESTEANUL,
Liberty and Tradition in Orthodox Monasticism

The living monastic tradition is that rich and common inheritance which monks and nuns have received from the past, continue to live in the present, and pass on to future generations. Tradition is the sap of monastic life. Without it, it is impossible to begin to understand this life's mystery.

The monastic tradition is an objective reality and hence authenticates all monastic living. The reason we monks speak of and show such reverence for tradition is that our life is incarnated, so to speak, in a living tradition and cannot be separated from it. This living tradition is the flow of life that has been handed over to us from the Sacred Scriptures, particularly the Gospels, the teachings of the apostles, the example of the early monks and nuns of the desert, and the continual monastic living throughout the centuries, with its ups and downs. Tradition is both continuity and direct link to our roots. Tradition is the Holy Spirit's inner dynamic that keeps the monastic life, like the Church, "ever ancient yet ever new."

However, as renowned monastic scholar Dom Jean Leclercq often used to remind us, there is Tradition and there are traditions. There is a great deal of misunderstanding in our time about these, and it is vitally important not to confuse them. The monastic tradition that we value is rooted in the Word of God, in the example of Jesus, and is that which the early monks and nuns inherited from the apostles and the first Christians. Tradition in this sense, conveying perennial Gospel values, remains of timeless value to us. Some of these values—like faith, prayer, conversion, humility, charity, simplicity, good works, obedience, and hospitality—are always valid no matter how they may be expressed in different cultures and at different times. Traditions, however, are another thing. Mere traditions are more or less culturally conditioned customs which originated at certain times and places. They are not essential to monastic life, as are the values that spring from the Gospel. Traditions of themselves are not necessarily bad, but it is important to see them in their historical contexts; otherwise, we may fall into danger of canonizing them. This distinction is particularly important for our time, with many people's great tendency toward fundamentalism.

To give one example of the difference between Tradition and traditions, let me speak of something greatly treasured in the life of a monastery, namely the Divine Offices. Up until the time of the last Ecumenical Council, the Offices were always celebrated in Latin and sung in the Gregorian chant. However, since the Council introduced the use of our vernacular languages into the Liturgy, many monasteries have opted likewise, finding that their mother tongue facilitates and strengthens their liturgical prayer. This option, in the light of Tradition, is completely valid, for those things which are important—prayer and the celebration of God's praises—are retained and hopefully enhanced. Thus, we see in this case that Tradition is upheld, while the traditions (Latin and the Gregorian chant) are replaced by other forms. Changes in minor traditions do not affect the nature of monastic life. It would be something altogether different, however, if the monasteries were to try to substitute prayer and the Offices themselves, which are intrinsic values in the monastic life. That would really be tampering with Tradition.

I do not wish to disparage Latin or the Gregorian chant, which are so dear to many monasteries and are, to some extent, used and retained here in our monastery. However, I think it is important to point out—even to those of us who retain such values—that these are part of traditions and not of Tradition. After all, the early monks in the desert, like Antony and Pachomius, did not know Latin, yet they were quite happy praising God in their own tongue.

Saint Antony, the Father of Monks, was called a true inheritor of the fire of Pentecost, for he was a man filled with the Holy Spirit. What we monks and nuns call the living monastic tradition is the precious pearl of the Gospel, an inheritance we have received from our ancient fathers and mothers, an inheritance which contains within itself life in the Holy Spirit, a life filled with fire and love, capable of being transmitted again and again to every generation.

> If we want to live as monks, we must try to understand
> what the monastic life really is. We must try to reach
> the springs from which that life flows. We must have
> some notions of our spiritual roots, that we may be
> better able to sink them deep into the soil.
>
> THOMAS MERTON, *The Monastic Journey*

St. Benedict

To prefer nothing to the love of Christ.
The Rule of St. Benedict, CHAPTER 4

The man of God Benedict of Norcia, blessed in name and by grace, is one of those remarkable saints whose influence affected the course of history. He is called the "Father and Patron of Europe" because his Rule contributed enormously to the shaping of Western civilization. St. Benedict was born in AD 480 in the small town of Norcia, north of Rome. During his adolescence he was sent by his parents to the great metropolis to pursue his studies. There in Rome Benedict encountered among the students a lifestyle of pleasure and vice and felt repelled by the ambiance. "Wishing to please God alone," as his biographer Gregory the Great points out, he decided to abandon Rome's worldly concerns and withdraw to the mountains of Subiaco, thirty miles east, where he embraced a solitary form of monastic life.

After several years of his strict solitude, a nearby community of monks approached him and requested that he become their abbot. Benedict accepted reluctantly, only to find later that this was a rebellious group of monks unwilling to accept any kind of reform—they went so far as to try to poison him. Benedict left the group and returned to his beloved solitude. Soon new disciples began to arrive, and he proceeded to instruct them by both word and example into the ways of monastic life. A new wave of hatred developed around him, and this time he decided to leave Subiaco permanently. He journeyed south with a few faithful disciples and settled in the area known as Monte Cassino, still inland, about halfway between Rome and Naples.

In the new monastery, Benedict was able to organize the monastic life of his monks in accordance with his *Rule for Monasteries*. This Rule, according to his biographer, "is so remarkable for its discretion and clarity of style, that anyone who wishes to know Benedict's character and life more precisely may find a complete account of his principles and practice in the ordinances of that Rule; for the saint cannot have taught otherwise than as he lived." St. Benedict died around AD 547, leaving his Rule as a testament of Gospel living for generations of monks to come.

The Rule of St. Benedict, full of wisdom and moderation and deeply rooted in the Gospels, seeks to balance the daily life of the monks between the practice of liturgical prayer, or *Opus Dei*, as St. Benedict called it; the private, prayerful reading of the Scriptures and the Fathers; manual labor to support the monastic community; and physical rest.

For St. Benedict the single aim of our Christian lives is to seek God and grow in the knowledge and love of Jesus Christ. The monk enters a monastery not to become a superior kind of being but simply to live his Christian life to the fullest. The monastery is, in Benedict's words, simply "a school in the Lord's service."

He counsels the monk to take the Gospel as his only guidance, thus treading the path that Christ has cleared for all of us (Prologue of the Rule). The monk, for St. Benedict, strives daily to become an ever humbler disciple who must "prefer nothing to the love of Christ." The monk thus undertakes daily the work of love, particularly through prayer, which becomes the living expression of his love for God and neighbor. Expressed through prayer, love draws the disciple closer to his only master, Christ, and also to all that Christ loves, that is, the entire world and every single being in it.

> We thank you, Lord Jesus Christ;
> In your immense love for us, you teach us
> Through the life and example of St. Benedict.
> Grant that by preferring your love above all things,
> We may be led to the fullness of life
> With the Father and the Holy Spirit.

The Rule of St. Benedict

*The Rule is always more than a code of life or a manual
of doctrine, although it is both of these. It is above all a
resumé of a spiritual experience that lies at the heart of
the monastic life. The principles of doctrines it evokes,
or the details of obedience which are recommended or
even imposed by it, have an inner power. This power is
an experience of the very life of God in Christ Jesus and
his Holy Spirit.*

*The letter of the Rule contains life within itself,
and this life can be awakened in the heart of the
disciple. Hence the importance of the very opening
words of the Rule: "Listen, my son."*
DOM ANDRÉ LOUF, *The Cistercian Way*

St. Benedict tells us in chapter 73, the last chapter of the Rule,
that he wrote "this little Rule for beginners." Since the sixth
century, innumerable monks and nuns have lived by it, and we
are still doing so in diverse cultural settings and across all conti-
nents. The Rule has survived the passing of time and has
inspired monks and nuns throughout the ages—proof of its
universal appeal, its wisdom, and certainly its timeless validity.
Thousands of books and articles have been written about the
Rule, by both monks and scholars who have studied the Rule
from every possible angle. Indeed, it never ceases to amaze me,
the great number of new books and commentaries on the
subject that appear every year.

Many young students come to our monastery and show
interest in monasticism. Some ask me why the Rule appeals to
persons in this technological twentieth century. What does a

sixth-century document have to say to people so removed in culture and time from St. Benedict?

The Rule can be appreciated for various aspects, but one that particularly appeals to me is its wise latitude in the way it encourages us monks to walk in the footsteps of the Gospel. The Rule tacitly acknowledges a certain pluralism, making general points instead of specific ones about many observances, allowing for creativity and improvement, where this is possible. The Rule is not limited to its original place and time; like the Gospels, from which it draws its inspiration, it has wisdom as alive and full of meaningful implications today as it was at the time the Rule was composed.

A second reason for the Rule's continuing appeal is its deep sense of personalism. Beginning with the first words of the Prologue, "Listen, my son," St. Benedict's great love for the reader is evident. It is to him that St. Benedict addresses the words of life of the Rule, thus passing on the grace, the wisdom, and the richness of his own experience. It is then up to the individual monk to embrace the Rule as a way of life, distilling wisdom day by day from it.

A third element in the Rule that retains a timeless appeal to monks is the perfect pattern it creates for the monastic day. The Rule prescribes an equal distribution of time among prayer, sacred reading and intellectual work, manual work, and rest, thus bringing into balance all the activities of the monastic day. St. Benedict was a genius in establishing through the Rule a way of life where the seasons of the earth, with their sequences of darkness and light, and the seasons of the Christian liturgy come into harmonious consonance, thus giving a dynamic balance and a healing rhythm to the monk's daily life.

The Rule, a perfect synthesis of what is best in the traditions of the East and the West, remains a living guide to the monastic journey. Every day we read a portion of the Rule in the monastery, and we find its teachings alive with meaning and purpose. When the postulant enters the novitiate, the monk in charge of training him daily opens the novice's eyes and heart to the truth and treasures contained in the Rule. Slowly, the novice learns to walk the path traced by the Rule, and he eventually finds there a quiet, hidden source of strength, sustaining and encouraging him throughout his inner journey. Through the reading and daily living out of the Rule, the presence and example of St. Benedict remains alive in the monastery and in the heart of the monk. The Rule is life-giving and consequently has the power to transmit this life from one generation of monks to another.

> In his Rule Saint Benedict did not seek to present a theory of the spiritual life, but simply to offer a practical program for persons wanting to live the Christian life fully. Nevertheless, all his specific directives are backed by clear insight into the essence and the mysteries of the spiritual life. This insight was deepened by years of intensive study of Holy Scripture, ecclesiastical writers, and monastic pioneers. It was confirmed and crowned by the experience of coming to know all the stages of the way to God in his own search and struggle.
>
> DOM EMMANUEL HEUFELDER, *The Way to God*

Lent

The Lenten spring has come.
The light of repentance is being offered to us.
Let us enter the season of Lent with joy,
Giving ourselves to spiritual strife, cleansing our soul
* and body,*
Controlling our passions as we limit our food,
And striving to live by the virtues inspired by the Spirit.
Let us persevere in our longing for God
So as to be worthy upon the completion of the forty days
To behold the most solemn passion of Christ,
And to feast with spiritual joy
In the most holy Passover of the Lord.

BYZANTINE LENTEN OFFICE

At the beginning of chapter 49 of the Rule, St. Benedict states in strong, clear terms that "the life of a monk ought always to have the character of a Lenten observance," thus emphasizing that for him Lent is not just one more liturgical season among many, but one that mirrors preeminently what the monk's life should be like at all times. He goes on to say that during Lent the monk should conduct his life with the greatest possible purity, avoiding the faults and negligence of the past. The monk will be able to accomplish this, St. Benedict tells him, by refraining from sin and devoting himself to prayer with tears, to holy reading, to repentance, and to abstinence. St. Benedict takes the Lenten observance so seriously that he bids his monks to see it as a program and model for all of their monastic life.

St. Benedict would not understand what Lent has become for many Christians today, trivialized to a time when we give up candy, cut down on television, or make a yearly confession. I find it sad to see that Lent has become reduced to such a poor shadow of the great significance it had during the first Christian centuries. Perhaps we can rediscover again its true meaning and experience anew its rich reality by incorporating into our lives some of the timeless principles that St. Benedict proposes to all of us as Lenten practices in the Rule.

The first principle that St. Benedict mentions, and this should be an obvious one, is "refraining from sin." Lent recalls for us, in particular, the forty days that Jesus spent in the desert doing battle with Satan, the tempter. Lent should be a time for us, too, to do battle, a time to fight not only the great temptations but, perhaps more importantly, our subtle faults, the seemingly small, habitual sins we consent to every day. Sometimes when we examine our consciences, we tend to look only for grave, serious sins and overlook the small ones that have become so encrusted in our personalities that we no longer recognize them for what they are. Lent is a propitious time to take inventory and a close look at our bare selves, to see the obstacles on our journey to God, things which should be eliminated from our lives. Lent provides us the occasion to work toward making radical changes in ourselves.

The second principle that St. Benedict proposes is for us to apply ourselves to prayer with tears. During the early days of Lent, the Gospel parable of the Pharisee and the publican (Luke 18: 9–14) is read to us in church. Jesus teaches that the Pharisee's prayer, filled with arrogance and pride, is not pleasing to God. In contrast, the humble prayer of the publican, a tax collector, who recognizes his sinfulness and makes appeal to God's mercy with inner tears, is the kind of prayer that touches the heart of God. Our Lenten prayer, like the publican's, ought then to be a humble and tearful prayer of compunction, a prayer of simplicity and trust, not in ourselves, but in the loving-kindness and tenderness of our God. This is the only form of prayer that can indeed bring us closer to God.

The third principle that St. Benedict mentions is holy reading. Lent is a season when the reading of the Sacred Scriptures, both the Old and the New Testaments, occupies a most important place in the monk's worship. The monk must not only apply himself to the reading of the Scriptures during his formal hours of prayer, but also make room for continuing its reading at other times and intervals. The monk, just as any other Christian, should develop a continual hunger, almost an addiction, for the Word of God, for through the Scriptures the Holy Spirit never ceases to speak to and educate us. As one of the early fathers poignantly said, "In the Scriptures Christ prays, weeps, and speaks directly to us." Lent is this wonderful, particularly well-suited time for reading and listening to the voice of God in his Word, thus entering into vital direct contact with him.

The fourth principle that St. Benedict emphasizes is at the heart of the Christian and, consequently, monastic life. St. Benedict speaks of repentance. At the threshold of Lent, when placing the ashes on our foreheads, the priest repeats the Gospel words, "Repent and believe in the Gospel" (Mark 1:15). Repentance, undertaken with humble sincerity and joy, symbolizes the beginning of a new life and is the necessary requirement

for making progress in this new life in Christ. Repentance, the work of the Holy Spirit in the innermost part of our hearts, implies a long, sustained spiritual effort. It is true that conversion and repentance are lifelong tasks, but Lent provides us with an exclusive period to work at it intensely. Lent is indeed "a school of repentance," as Father Schememann beautifully wrote, and we receive it every year as a gift from God, a time to deepen our faith and to reevaluate and change our lives.

The last principle mentioned by St. Benedict, abstinence from food, long associated with Lent, is not solely a Christian or monastic practice. A well-known practice in non-Christian religions, fasting is also sometimes practiced in secular society for purely medical, dietary, or therapeutic reasons. For the Christian, however, fasting from food bears a special connotation, being rooted in the example of Christ, who fasted forty days and forty nights (Matthew 4:2). Christ used fasting, and encouraged his followers to practice fasting, as a way of learning the self-control and personal restraint we need to keep a humble and wise perspective on our Christian life. Through the painful experience of hunger, we come to the realization of our human limitations and of our utter dependence on God. Fasting is not only a physical activity but primarily a spiritual one. Through it we undergo, during our often tedious Lenten days, a process of self-emptying, of self-dying. This process can be painful and wearying, but when carried out under the guidance of the Holy Spirit, it becomes life-giving and the source of powerful grace in our individual lives. For the Christian, fasting is never disconnected from prayer and concentration on God, for the one concluding lesson that we can all get from fasting is the awareness that it deepens in us, and feeds, a tremendous longing, need, and hunger for God.

St. Benedict, having artfully mastered the practice of these Lenten observances in the example of his own life, encourages the disciple to do the same in the joy of the Holy Spirit, undertaking his monastic journey toward the feast of Easter with the joy of spiritual desire. Easter then becomes the culmination and the fulfillment of all of one's spiritual desires, the blossoming of new life in joy by the power of the Resurrection of Christ.

> Lent is a journey, a pilgrimage! Yet, as we begin it, as we make the first step into the "bright sadness" of Lent, we see—far away—the destination. It is the joy of Easter; it is the entrance into the glory of the Kingdom. And it is the vision, the foretaste of Easter, that make Lent's sadness bright and our Lenten effort a "spiritual spring."
>
> Fr. Alexander Schememann, *Great Lent*

St. Mary of Egypt

The power of your cross, O Christ,
Has worked wonders,
For even the woman who was once a harlot
Chose the ascetic monastic way.
Casting aside her weakness,
Bravely she opposed the devil;
And having gained the prize of victory,
She intercedes for the salvation of our souls.
    "Lenten Triodon," Canon of St. Mary of Egypt

The life of St. Mary of Egypt is not only an obvious ascetic
triumph, a triumph of love, but also a triumph over any
preconceived notions of holiness.
                    Mother Thekla, *IKONS*

St. Mary of Egypt was one of those early desert mothers who
has a timeless appeal to all those who seek God by way of the
monastic life. Mary was a fifth-century prostitute from
Alexandria who spent the early part of her life corrupting the
young men of Egypt. She enjoyed entertaining all those who
came her way, but she refused payment. Pleasure was the only
motivation for her behavior.

One day she decided to join a group of pilgrims who were
going from Cairo to the city of Jerusalem to celebrate the feast
of the Holy Cross. With great curiosity she followed the
pilgrims to the Church of the Holy Cross, wanting very much
to see the true Cross. However, a mysterious force somehow
prevented her from entering the church every time she tried to
do it. While the crowd of pilgrims could move forward, she felt

paralyzed and couldn't move. Bewildered and saddened by her hopeless attempts to enter the church and glimpse the true Cross and feeling utterly rejected, she turned to an icon of the Mother of God and prayed for help:

> O ever blessed Virgin and Lady, you gave birth to the Word of God in the flesh. I know that it is not proper for me, foul and corrupt, to gaze upon your holy icon, O most pure one! But if, as I have heard, God became man, born of you, to call sinners to repentance, help me in my distress, for I have no one to help me. Command the entrance into the church to be opened to me; do not let me be deprived of gazing upon the tree on which God in the flesh, born of you, was nailed and shed his own blood to redeem me. I call upon you to be my guarantor before your son that never again shall I defile this body with shameful fornication, but as soon as I venerate the tree of the Cross, immediately after I shall renounce the world and all its vanities, and I shall go wherever you, the guarantor of my salvation, order me to go and lead me.

And as Mary was praying to the Mother of God with such earnestness and tears, she received the grace to move forward to the Cross of Christ, then forward to the River Jordan and forward into the desert, where the Mother of God led her, as Mother Thekla explains in *IKONS,* "forward into year after year of icy cold and burning heat, of temptation and carnal longing, of fear and despair, and, finally, of the peace above all understanding."

The example of the holiness of St. Mary of Egypt, whose feast is celebrated on April 2, usually in the middle of our Lenten observance, has deep significance for all those who follow the monastic way. Her life portrays the dramatic tale of the work of lust turned into the work of love by the mystery of grace and repentance. For the Christian who embraces the monastic state and receives the "habit of repentance," as the ancient monks used to call the monastic garb, it is the abiding conviction that humble repentance is his ordinary, real, and only way to God. Repentance is an illumination and a grace, a humble attitude of heart and mind, that brings healing and inner freedom to all those who, moved by the Holy Spirit, embrace it wholeheartedly as a genuine gift from God.

The life of St. Mary of Egypt is read every year in the Offices of the fifth Sunday of Lent in the Eastern churches and monasteries.

Open to me the gates of repentance, O Giver of life;
For my spirit rises early to pray towards your holy
     temple,
Bearing the temple of my body all defiled;
But in your compassion, purify me by the loving-
     kindness of your mercy.

Lead me on the paths of salvation, O Mother of God;
For I have profaned my soul with shameful sins,
And have wasted my life in laziness.
But by your intercession, deliver me from all impurity.

When I think of the many evil things I have done,
     wretch that I am,
I tremble at the fearful day of judgment.
But trusting in your loving-kindness, like David I cry
     to you:
Have mercy on me, O God, according to your great
     mercy.

"LENTEN TROPARIA"

Easter

This is the day of the Resurrection,
Let us be illumined, O Christian people,
For this is the day of the sacred Passover of the Lord.
Come, and let us drink of the new river,
Not brought forth from a barren stone,
But from the fount of life
That springs forth from the sepulchre of Christ the Lord.
St. John Damascene, "Easter Canon"

For the monk in the monastery or hermitage, as for other
Christians at home, the joyful festival of the Resurrection of the
Lord follows the Lenten period of prayer, fasting, and quiet
introspection. But just as we are about to arrive at the celebration of this glorious festival, we spend the last days of Holy
Week at the foot of the Cross with Our Lady, in mournful
remembrance of the pain and suffering that her son Jesus under-
went for our sake. These are very quiet days in the monastery,
for we carry the heavy burden of grief in our hearts. Good
Friday is a day of black fast, when not even dairy products are
allowed, and the fare of the monk is reduced to bread and water,
or other liquids like tea or coffee. After the stark afternoon
Liturgy of Christ's Passion, we retire to our cells for more
prayer, reading, and meditation. At night, before going to
rest, we recite compline and sing the Stabat Mater in a mournful
Gregorian chant melody that recalls Mary's solitude in suffering
as she wept for her son at the foot of the cross.

Holy Saturday follows, called "the most blessed Sabbath
on which Christ sleeps," by the Liturgy. I am particularly fond
of Holy Saturday. In a way, it is even quieter than Good Friday,

since no liturgy is celebrated, but we share both in the sorrow of the Passion and burial of Jesus and in the anticipated joy of the Resurrection. An Eastern Byzantine text poignantly conveys the mystery of Holy Saturday:

> O happy tomb! You received within yourself
> the Creator and the Author of life.
> O strange wonder! He who dwells on high
> is sealed beneath the earth with his own consent.

The stillness, the deep silence, and the peace we experience on Holy Saturday, keeping watch by the tomb of Christ, is perhaps the best preparation for the explosive, all-powerful joy of the Resurrection. Very often in life, we are likewise led through loss and sorrow to a new phase of peace and understanding that ultimately culminates in deep joy.

At the end of Holy Saturday, very late and in the midst of the darkness of night, the Paschal Vigil quietly begins with the blessing of the new fire from which the Paschal Candle is lit. A procession forms, and the monks and the faithful, with lighted

candles in their hands, solemnly follow the Paschal Candle into
the dark church. There the Exultet, the glorious proclamation of
the Resurrection of Christ, is announced in song to the whole
world. It is a particularly moving moment in the Easter Liturgy
to hear the haunting Gregorian melody, in perfect unison with
the text, proclaim the wonders of God in the Resurrection.
After the singing of the Exultet, the night vigil proceeds with
psalms, and antiphons sung in between. Following the readings
we reach the climax of our Easter Vigil, the solemn celebration
of the Eucharist banquet. At the beginning of the Eucharist, the
celebrant intones the Gloria. As the monks sing the beautiful
Gregorian chant from the Mass I *Lux et origo* of paschaltime,
the bells of the monastery peel out in joy, announcing
throughout our hills and valleys the glad tidings of the
Resurrection.

At the end of Mass, our Easter lamb, the youngest of our
flock and a symbol of Christ, the immolated Lamb of God, is
blessed with the new Easter water, then taken back to the sheep-
fold. Easter is a feast when all creation rejoices in the
Resurrection of the Creator of all life, so the animals, the plants,
and the flowers of the monastery all partake in this rejoicing.

I am always so glad to see the myriad daffodils on the
monastic property bloom in such profusion during Eastertide.
After the blessing of the lamb, a long period of thanksgiving and
prayer follows, which allows the monk to quietly absorb the
great mystery just commemorated. Before we retire for a few
hours of rest, each monk receives a bottle of newly blessed
Easter water, which he carries into his monastic cell and which
will last him until the following Easter.

In the early evening of Easter Sunday, the solemn Vespers
of the Resurrection are sung in the monastery chapel. The
Vespers begin with the hymn "Ad Coenam Agni Providi,"
which I consider one of the most beautiful in the entire
Gregorian repertory. After the hymn the exquisite antiphons of

the feast with their respective psalms are sung, relating to us once more the biblical details of the Resurrection. Our solemn Vespers reaches its climatic point with the proclamation of the Gospel account of Jesus' appearance to the disciples on that first Easter evening. First the book of the Gospels and the paschal candle, symbols of Christ, are incensed; then the beautiful account is read. A long silence follows the reading. One can feel the immediacy of the Lord's risen presence. Vespers concludes, as it always does, with the solemn singing of the Magnificat, Mary's song of praise to God for his great wonders.

It is of no small significance that the yearly celebration of Lent, Holy Week, and Easter coincides with the arrival of spring. Lent allows us to face all the grim aspects of our life and points us toward the joyful hope of new Easter life. In monasteries, where the Lenten practice of fasting and penance tends to be rather sober in nature, our joy in the Resurrection knows no bounds. It is the most thrilling and uplifting experience of the liturgical year. The bells ring with alleluias; the chapel is filled with fresh flowers and bright lights; the chant echoes the joy of Christ's Resurrection, as both monks and nuns greet one another with the traditional "Christ is risen" and its reply, "Indeed, he is risen." Spring and Easter are almost synonymous. The new life of spring, such as the flowers springing up in our gardens, is a symbol fully realized in the springing up of divine life in the inner depths of our hearts. The season of spring and the mystery of Easter, celebrated together, bring us from sorrow and death to the affirmation of hope and the experience of the renewal of life in our daily existence.

> God send us the springtime lamb
> minted and tied in thyme
> and call us home, and bid us eat
> and praise your name.
>   ANNIE DILLARD, FROM "FEAST DAYS"

Spring Gardening

Behind the abbey, and within the wall of the cloister,
there is a wide level of ground: here there is an orchard,
with a great many different fruit trees, quite like a
small wood. It is close to the infirmary, and is very
comforting to the monks, providing a wide promenade
for those who want to walk, and a pleasant resting place
for those who prefer to rest. Where the orchard leaves
off, the garden begins, divided into several beds, or still
better cut up by little canals. . . . The water fulfills the
double purpose of nourishing the fish and watering the
vegetables.

ANONYMOUS, FRENCH MANUSCRIPT, TWELFTH CENTURY

The Lord God then "took the man and settled him in the garden of Eden to cultivate and take care of it" (Genesis 2:15). At the beginning of time, gardening was recognized as part of God's mandate to man to care for the Earth. The early monks in the Egyptian desert took to heart this Biblical command, becoming avid gardeners as well as watchful stewards of the land entrusted to them. The idea of the garden was dearly loved by them, for it also enabled them to recreate the paradise man and woman had once shared with God. These early monks went on to elaborate the principles of monastic gardening in the same way and at the same time that they elaborated the other principles of monastic life.

An early life of St. Antony, written by his friend St. Hilarion, describes Antony's little garden: "These vines and these little trees did he plant; the pool did he contrive, with much labor for the watering of his garden; with his rake did he break up the earth for many years." St. Antony cultivated his garden to provide food for himself and to share the rest with his neighbors, especially the poor, as the Gospel commands. Since gardening had such a prominent place in monasteries, it is not surprising that the two patron saints of gardening were monks, St. Phocas and St. Fiacre, who are always portrayed with their spade, shovel, or rake.

An early medieval manuscript that has survived into our own day shows a plan, drawn up for the Benedictine abbey of St. Gall in the ninth century, of an ideal monastery, with its dependencies and gardens. There we discover the cloister, with its traditional garden, the physician's herb garden near the infirmary, and the large garden to feed the monastic community. Attached to this large garden was the gardener's garden. The monks grew fruits and vegetables, flowers and vines, flavoring and healing herbs, and plants that provided dyes, inks, and incense for the monastery.

This long gardening tradition continues today; it is still a thoroughly monastic occupation. In early spring, as soon as the soil is workable and warm, I begin work in our enclave's gardens. Before the enjoyable task of planting, there is the yearly cleanup and raking of winter's debris. Then I plant the seeds for later harvest: lettuce, arugula, spinach, swiss chard, radishes, and peas are some of these first. An early start expedites germination. And the sooner the plants begin to grow, the quicker they develop strong root systems, which collect the soil, moisture, and nutrients necessary to good health and excellent yields. Careful gardeners—and we try to be such, as monks—must be vigilant at this stage to ensure that seedlings are not killed by a late frost, which here can occur as late as the middle of May. (Gardeners here do not set out tomatoes, peppers, eggplants, and cucumbers before the Memorial Day weekend.)

Gardening within a monastery is both a task and an art, and it's something we only gradually begin to fathom in the early years of our monastic life. The more experienced gardener monks teach us to start slowly. They instruct us on how to improve our soil with compost and other amendments, knowing well that this will have a profound effect on the variety of plants we grow. I learned early, as well, to let Mother Nature be our guide. Her signals often indicate the propitious time for many garden chores. For instance, when the crocus is in bloom, we begin cleaning up winter's debris. When the forsythia begins to bloom, we prune the roses, evergreens, and plants that have been damaged by the winter. When the soil warms up, we begin to divide and transplant the perennials.

Spring gardening occupies a special place in the heart of the monk, for it usually coincides with Easter, which is also the feast of our monastery. Spring gardening nurtures hope in the monk, then fulfills the promise of new life when all creation is renewed by the power of Christ's Resurrection.

> Though a life of retreat offers various joys,
> none, I think, will compare with the time one employs
> in the study of herbs, or in striving to gain
> some practical knowledge of nature's domain.
> Get a garden! What kind you may get matters not.
> WALAFRID-STRABO, *Hortulus,*
> LATIN MANUSCRIPT, NINTH CENTURY

Pentecost

O Heavenly King, the Comforter, the Spirit of Truth,
Who are everywhere and fill all things,
Treasury of blessings, and Giver of life!
Come and abide in us,
Cleanse us from all our sins,
And save our souls, O Good One!

BYZANTINE PRAYER TO THE HOLY SPIRIT

The Thursday which follows the fifth Sunday after Easter is the day when monasteries celebrate the feast of the Ascension of the Lord into heaven. Jesus, having fulfilled his earthly mission, went to the Mount of Olives, took leave of his mother and the disciples, and ascended from there to his Father in heaven. It was his final act on this earth, but it was an act that opens to us, his followers, endless possibilities, for Jesus did not return to the Father alone. Through the mystery of the Incarnation, Jesus assumed all of humanity into himself, and now all of us are part of him. As the doors of the kingdom of heaven opened wide to receive the triumphant Lord, the whole of redeemed humanity was also being received and accepted by the Father. The feast of the Ascension celebrates not only Jesus' glorification by the Father, but also the Father's acceptance of each one of us. Jesus opens heaven to us, makes it our destination and permanent home, where one day we will also be received into the warm embrace of a loving Father.

While we are celebrating the Ascension, the liturgical chants and readings are already making subtle allusions to the Holy Spirit, the Comforter, whom Jesus will send. The Ascension in a sense is a necessary prelude to Pentecost.

The Book of Acts recounts the Pentecost event: "When Pentecost day came around, they had all met in one room, when suddenly they heard what sounded like a powerful wind from heaven, the noise of which filled the entire house in which they were sitting; and something appeared to them that seemed like tongues of fire; these separated and came to rest on the head of each of them. They were all filled with the Holy Spirit" (2:1–4).

Pentecost is a time of fruitfulness, of fullness, of completion. The Holy Spirit is being given to us to continue on earth the work Jesus started. At Pentecost the Holy Spirit appears in the forms of wind and fire, two powerful elements of life on our planet. Pentecost takes place at the time of transition from spring to summer. Summer, with its intense mixture of wind and fire, is a symbolic season of the Holy Spirit, who is the life-giver and the maker of all things new. The heat of summer clothes with exuberant colors the flowers in our gardens and gives magnificent texture and taste to our fruits and vegetables. The fire of the Holy Spirit similarly clothes our souls with colors of grace and makes us taste the sweetness of divine life with God.

Monks throughout the ages have had a special affinity and place in their lives for the Holy Spirit. St. Seraphim of Sarov affirms that "the whole purpose of the Christian life consists in the acquisition of the Holy Spirit." Monks remind themselves daily of the truth of this teaching and try to attune themselves to the whispers of this mysterious presence who dwells within them, who they know to be the Spirit of God. Without him, monks can do nothing, and he alone can bring a personal monastic life out of chaos into a perfectly unified and harmonious whole. The Holy Spirit upholds the life of God deep within each of us, and his power is the force that mysteriously transforms our lives.

> If the soul keeps far away from all discourse in words, from all disorder and human disturbance, the Spirit of God will come in to her, and she who was barren will be fruitful.
>
> Abba Poeman, *The Sayings of the Desert Fathers*

Summer

Aspects of
Monastic Life

Living Faith

*"I tell you solemnly, if your faith were the size of a
mustard seed you could say to this mountain, 'Move
from here to there,' and it would move; nothing would
be impossible for you."*

MATTHEW 17:20

Faith is the point of all departure when one embarks upon the
adventure of the monastic life. Faith, according to the Gospels,
is the one requirement Jesus makes of his disciples in order
that they accomplish God's actions in their midst. It is a very
uplifting joy to read the many Gospel passages where Jesus
attributes the performance of God's wonders to the faith of
those who ask for it. To mention just a few, there are the stories
of the paralytic lowered through the roof (Luke 5:17–26), the
cure of the woman with a hemorrhage and the daughter of Jairus
raised to life (Mark 5:21–42), and the healing of the daughter of
the Canaanite woman (Matthew 15:21–28). It is also worthwhile
to give serious consideration to the rebukes Jesus makes to
those of little or no faith and how this lack of faith on our part
impedes the accomplishment of God's work in us. See the
account of the calming of the storm (Mark 4:35–41), the parable
of the unscrupulous judge and the importunate widow (Luke
18:1–8), and the cursing of the barren fig tree (Matthew
21:18–22).

But what is faith? The new *Catechism of the Catholic
Church* defines it as "the submission of our intellect and our will
to God." It is our human response to the God who reveals
himself to us and calls us to fellowship with him. What St. Paul
calls "the obedience of faith" (Romans 1:5), according to the

new Catechism, means "to submit freely to the word that has been heard, because its truth is guaranteed by God, who is truth itself."

Faith ultimately is a gift from God—a gift that allows us to place our intellect, our knowledge, ourselves, and our entire lives into the hands of God, the sole reason for our being and living. The moment the gift of faith is bestowed on us, it changes our lives dramatically. It makes all the difference in the world. Faith remains a great mystery, a mystery that seems easier to be experienced by the believer than to be explained to one who has no faith. Through the reality of faith, Christ becomes present in our lives. Through the experience of faith, we sense the power of the Holy Spirit at work in us, changing those things in our lives which are not pleasing to God, and transforming us more and more into the image of Jesus, the Father's beloved Son.

The new Catechism proposes Mary, the Mother of God, as a living example of what "obedience of faith" means. Only by appreciating the mystery of her faith can we understand Mary's acceptance of the archangel Gabriel's message and her complete submission to God's will. Deep in her heart she believed that

"'nothing is impossible to God'" (Luke 1:37), and she gave her assent, which forever changed the course of the world. The great mystery of the Incarnation was accomplished in a humble hand-maid, whose faith and humility captivated the heart of God himself. Because of her deep faith in God's promises, we Christians of every generation honor her and call her blessed.

Faith is truly a mysterious thing. As with any gift, we have the freedom to accept or reject it. If we accept it and assent to God's plans for us, as Mary did in Nazareth, then we can expect some deep surprises ahead. Mary's faith accepted joyfully the good tidings of the Annunciation. This same faith that allowed her to trust God for who he is, however, made her also accept his will during the pains of the Crucifixion, when much was asked of her son—and of her, as well, standing at the foot of the Cross. She did not understand it all, but she never questioned God, and she knew that in receiving and accepting the gift of faith, there could also be a price to pay.

Doubts may assail us from time to time, as they did, for example, the saints. St. Therese of Lisieux, a nineteenth-century Carmelite nun, suffered enormous doubts and temptations against faith on her deathbed. Though utterly frustrated in a human way, she had complete trust in the Word of the Lord and accepted what it had in store for her. Likewise, in our inner journey, we must not succumb in our dark hours of doubt and contradictions, but press on, with our faith firmly grounded in the promise of God's Word. There alone lies the solution.

God gives us this life on earth so that we may learn to believe, learn to believe him and his only Son, Jesus, whom he sent into this world to save us. Everything that happens in our daily lives should make us grow deeper and lead us further into this belief. Whatever our problems and difficulties are, whatever fears and limitations we face daily, through the eyes of faith we shall be able to sense the saving power of God at work in our lives. Faith will show us that our sinfulness, our poverty, and our powerlessness are not obstacles to the workings of God's grace in us. Neither darkness nor terror will ever again overtake us, for we shall be illuminated by the truth and the vision of God, which is incompatible with all darkness.

> What treasures of peace, love, and wisdom
> You store up, O Lord, for those who believe in You.
> You fill them with trust and confidence,
> And you shelter them under the shadow of your
>   wings.
> Be merciful, to us, O Lord,
> And grant us also the same faith,
> That we may know the true joy of knowing You
> And your only begotten Son, whom you sent to us,
> Our Lord Jesus Christ.

The Desert:
The Quest for the Absolute

Christ's three answers to Satan resounded in the silence of the desert; it was therefore here that the monks came in order to hear them again and to receive them as the rule of their monastic life.

PAUL EVDOKIMOV, *The Struggle with God*

Christian monastic life had its humble origin in the desert. The first monks went to the desert to seek God and to pursue a life of union with him. The desert was a special place, for it was there, according to Biblical accounts, that God had revealed himself in all his glory. In the desert at Mount Sinai, God revealed his name to Moses. During the forty years in the desert, the Lord fed his people with manna from above and gave them water from a rock. It was also in the desert of Sinai that the prophet Elias met God and entered into dialogue with him.

In the New Testament, we see that John the Baptist went to the desert to prepare there the way for the Lord. Later, Jesus himself, led by the Holy Spirit, retired to the desert to prepare for the mission for which his Father had sent him. To the desert he returned again and again, to rest and to pray, during the three years of his ministry. And it was in the desert at Mount Tabor, shortly before his Passion, that he lifted for a short time the veil of his humanity and revealed to his apostles the splendor of his divinity.

By retiring to the desert, the early monks and nuns were not primarily seeking to renounce all human fellowship. Instead, their aim was to seek God unhindered by the cares of the worldly society of their day. There is no denying that the times

of the desert fathers were turbulent and confusing, not unlike our own time, and not just in civil society but also in the Church of God. In the midst of all this confusion, the clear message of the Gospels often became blurred and distorted. The early monks and nuns, following the example of the apostles and martyrs, refused to compromise with the world. They instead sought refuge in the desert, where they could clearly hear the Word of God and live by it, with all its consequences. In this early desert adventure, the monastic movement originated, and it has ever since been shaped and influenced by it. The call to the solitude of the desert is a constant element in the monastic heart.

However, one thing the desert fathers and mothers, in their deep realism, would teach us today is that the desert does not always need to be a geographical place. It can also be found in the solitude and innermost spaces of our hearts. What counts is our inner attitude. Prayer was the central activity of the desert life, and we can also pray anywhere by heeding the Gospel's words: "When you pray, go to your private room and, when you have shut the door, pray to your Father who is in that secret place" (Matthew 6:6). Continual, unceasing prayer, coupled with the daily practice of Christian virtues: charity, humility, obedience, asceticism—these were the ideals for which the desert monks strove in their desert solitude, and which remain valid for monks and Christians of all persuasions today. Ultimately, it means taking both the Gospel and our Christian life seriously.

Faithful to this early monastic desert experience, many monasteries are established in isolated places. Today monks often retire for periods of time to a hermitage or take a once-a-week "desert day" in complete solitude, where we are given the opportunity to confront the absolute God and the crude reality of our own nakedness. It is an immense help in the spiritual life. This experience of the desert is so vital to all Christian life that monks and nuns hospitably allow their fellow Christians, and often non-Christians, to partake of the prayer, silence, and solitude of our monasteries.

> *The desert is fundamentally a state of insecurity.*
> *When lost in the desert, this place offers man one*
> *objective situation, only one solution: to look to God*
> *who redeems us and to wait with complete trust upon*
> *him, to abide by an absolute and radical confidence in*
> *God alone.*
>
> Fr. Edward Schillebeeckx, O.P.

The Monastery

The paths leading to the monastery are diverse. But one day they will converge and form a single way, meeting in him who said, "I am the Way," and "No one can come to the Father except through me." The Christian who becomes a monk is seeking no other way than this. What he makes his own is what he has seen and heard in the words and deeds of Jesus. As St. Benedict said in the Prologue to his Rule for monasteries, "Let us set out on this way with the Gospel for our guide. . . ." In saying this, St. Benedict is saying no more than St. John, who said, "We must live the same kind of life that Christ lived."

Dom André Louf, *The Cistercian Way*

St. Benedict conceived the purpose of a monastery to be "a school in the Lord's service," that is to say, a school of life where the monk is taught to live by the teachings of the Gospel and is shown the path to salvation. The monastery is the training ground where the monk learns to orient his whole life toward rendering fitting service to the Lord. A monastery, as all schools are, is located in a definite place, and it comprises a church and buildings like a dormitory or cells, cloister, refectory, library, scriptorium, chapter room, parlors, and workrooms. There are usually also gardens, orchards, and farm buildings within the monastic enclosure. The monastery is a home to the monk, and by his vow of stability, he becomes permanently attached to this home, to his monastic community, and to the physical locality, where he will spend the rest of his days in God's service.

A monastery is a school where the monk is taught different subjects:

School of Prayer   A monastery is a place where the monk learns to seek after the living God. Prayer is the natural expression of this seeking, so the monk cultivates the art of prayer as his life's sole reason. Several times during the day, the monk is summoned by bells to the Oratory to sing the Opus Dei, the praises of God. Prolonged periods are given to private, solitary prayer. Continual prayer is sought by frequent recourse to the Prayer of the Name of Jesus.

School of Silence   The deep monastic silence is the ordinary climate where the monk reads, studies, and is nourished by the Word of God. The silence of a monastery helps to create a unique quality of life, a creative stillness in which the monk and those who share his life are able to experience God and to begin to grasp the mystery of their existence.

School of Work   In imitation of the life of Christ, the monk leads a simple, poor, and laborious life. The monk lives from the work of his hands, which allows him to live in solidarity with his fellow human beings, especially the poor and the oppressed. The monk's work is connected with the flow of the seasons and the rhythm of creation. Special reverence is given to the cultivation of the land and to animal farming. Conservation, recycling, frugality, and austerity are aspects of the monastic lesson of cooperation with and utmost respect for the mystery of God's creation.

School of Fraternal Life   Guided by the Rule, the monastic community is a stable family unit centered around the abbot, who "is believed to be the representative of Christ in the monastery." As the early Christians were, the monastic community strives to be "united, heart and soul" (Acts 4:32).

School of Conversion to Christ   Moved by the Holy Spirit and desiring to live in closer communion with Christ, the monk vows obedience, conversion, and stability to a particular monastery. There he seeks to imitate the hidden life of Christ through obedience, humility, prayer, work, fasting, and keeping vigils. The monk denies himself daily in order to follow Christ (Rule, chapter 4).

School of the Heart St. Benedict, taking after St. John Cassian and the early monastic tradition, envisions the monastic ideal as "seeking God with purity of heart." Jesus makes purity of heart one of the Beatitudes: "Blessed are the pure of heart, for they shall see God" (Matthew 5:8, Revised Standard Version). The monk begins here and now to behold the face of God, which he will see for all eternity. Purity of heart is a necessary condition for union with God and, consequently, for progress in the life of prayer. Purity of heart allows the monk to be docile and receptive to the inspirations of the Holy Spirit and his gift of wisdom, and it gives the monk intuition and a foretaste of divine things.

School of Peace "Pax" is the motto of every Benedictine monastery. It expresses perfectly the ideal of monastic life according to St. Benedict, for whom the monastery is an abode of peace, for there dwell those who seek the God of peace. The monk strives daily for the harmony and the organic unity which existed at the beginning of creation.

School of Learning, Culture, and the Arts The tradition of scholarship and culture among the Benedictines is well known, and its decisive influence in the shaping of civilization in Europe has been established. Faithfully guarding the patrimony of this tradition, the monastery zealously encourages the monk in the "love of learning" and the appreciation and development of culture. Not only is the monk encouraged to study, to work, and to do research, he is also encouraged to enter into dialogue with the many scholars, scientists, artists, craftsmen, writers, and workers who come to the monastery, attracted by the values, wisdom, and unity of the monastic life. The cultivation of beauty and the arts, especially in its relation to the worship of

God, takes a preeminent place in a monastery. Among the art forms, music has particular importance, for it is integrated in the daily prayers.

School of Service   Through the ancient practice of monastic hospitality, the monk shares his life with his fellow men. According to the monastic tradition, the doors of a monastery are to be open to all who seek the peace of God. Amidst the agitation, the noise, and the fast pace of daily living, monasteries offer "spaces of silence" and also the "experience of the desert" so vital for all those wishing to enter into living contact with Christ and renew their friendship with him.

> St. Benedict says that it must be ascertained of a novice whether he is truly seeking God, and he describes the monastery as a school in the Lord's service. And indeed, the monk may well be likened to a student engaged in the most thrilling piece of research work which could be imagined. He cannot tell where it will lead him. Sometimes it is as if he is out on a wide uncharted sea, knowing that though he sees no shore in sight, yet his course is straight and clear before him, because God is the sovereign owner of ship and shore and sea.
>
> SISTER KATHERINE, *A Threefold Cord*

The Abbot:
The Father in the Monastery

> *To be worthy to govern a monastery an abbot should*
> *always remember what he is called and carry out his*
> *high calling in his everyday life. He is believed to hold*
> *the place of Christ in the monastery, since he is*
> *addressed by the title applied to Christ, as the Apostle*
> *indicates: You have received the spirit of adoption of*
> *sons by which we cry, Abba, Father. Therefore, the*
> *abbot must never teach or decree or command anything*
> *that would deviate from the Lord's instructions.*
>
> RULE OF ST. BENEDICT, CHAPTER 2

St. Benedict sees the monastery as "a school in the Lord's service" where the monk comes to be formed, and the monastic community as a real, stable family centered around the abbot, the father of the community. He envisions in the community the harmony of an ideal family, where the brethren mutually support each other and where the father leads them wisely and prudently in their quest for God.

In the monastic tradition, the role of the abbot is much more than just the juridical figure the superior is in other religious communities. In fact, there is no parallel there. For St. Benedict the abbot "takes the place of Christ" in the community, and it is around him that the stable fraternal relationships of the monastic family are built. With his example and teaching, the abbot encourages the monks to love one another as brothers, practicing charity in forbearance, patience, and mutual respect. Everything done in the monastery is under his direction and with his consent.

St. Benedict's conception of the monastic community as a family helps us understand the Benedictine vow of stability. Because the monk is part of a permanent, concrete family, he vows stability to the particular monastery of his profession until death. This helps the monk to surrender "mobility"—one of the physical expressions of pride, independence, and self-will—to the healing yoke of obedience. Stability to a particular monastic family brings to the monk's heart the gifts of security, inner peace, and joy in the Holy Spirit.

St. Benedict, being both a very spiritual and a practical man, counsels the abbot to form and instruct the monastic community not only with words but also by his good behavior. In the Rule he prescribes, "Furthermore, anyone who receives the name of abbot is to lead his disciples by a twofold teaching; he must point out to them all that is good and holy more by example than by words, proposing the commandments of the Lord to receptive disciples with words, but demonstrating God's instructions to the stubborn and the dull by a living example" (chapter 2). St. Benedict makes it abundantly clear that the abbot must be to his disciples a living example of holiness, and he assures the abbot that his example of holiness and fidelity to Christ at the end would do more for the spiritual welfare of the brethren than all the sermons preached with the most gifted eloquence.

> Saint Benedict laid the obligation on all, brothers and abbot, to follow the Rule. At all times and especially in periods of universal decline, the community and the abbot have no better safeguard than a religious respect for an untouchable rule. An abbot is nothing without a rule.
>
> DOM ADALBERT DE VOGÜE, *The Rule of St. Benedict*

Obedience

Jesus said: "My food is to do the will of the one who sent me, and to complete his work."
                                        JOHN 4:34

The function of faith in obedience is to make the monk see it is God himself whom he obeys each and every time he answers a bell, fulfills a request favor, carries out a wish or command of a superior or another brother. Faith keeps the monk sensitive to God's voice speaking through his spokesmen.
                    DOM WILFRED TUNINK, *Vision of Peace*

The monk's obedience is based on Jesus' attitude toward his Father. Jesus' entrance into the world was marked by "Behold, I come to do your will," and his daily prayer was "Your will be done." The monastic concept of obedience is not simply legalistic, but one of complete openness and fidelity to the will of the Father as it reveals itself in the monk's very ordinary daily life. Following the example of the Lord, the monk promises to remain obedient "even unto death" in the monastery. This obedience in monastic life implies fidelity and obedience to the will of God, to the Rule and the monastic tradition, to the father of the community, and to one another.

To obey is to commit oneself to the state of being a servant as Christ was, and thus to make a total offering of oneself.
                    DOM ANDRE LAUF, *The Cistercian Way*

Humility

Just as one cannot build a ship unless one has some nails,
so it is impossible to be saved without humility.
　　　AMMA SYNCLETICA, *The Sayings of the Desert Fathers*

It is no great thing to be with God in your thoughts,
but it is a great thing to see yourself as inferior to all
creatures. It is this, coupled with hard work, that leads
to humility.
　　　ABBA SISOES, *The Sayings of the Desert Fathers*

"This is what Yahweh asks of you: only this, to act justly, to love
tenderly and to walk humbly with your God" (Micah 6:8). This
text from the Old Testament prophet sums up St. Benedict's
teaching on humility, and it could be proposed to all monks as
the program of the monastic life. If St. Benedict places such
emphasis on the role of humility in the monks' lives, it is because
the Gospels themselves teach and require it of all Christians.
Humility of spirit is an essential attitude that Jesus demands from
all his followers. Even when we perform good deeds, the Gospel
bids us to remember that we are nothing but "useless servants."

　　The emphasis on humility in monastic life is one of those
aspects that makes monasticism so countercultural. Our
present-day culture fosters self-assertion, self-exaltation, self-
pride, and ultimately self-glorification. The glory is no longer
given to God but to the self. The need for humility is replaced
by the sin of pride.

　　In contrast, Jesus teaches in the story of the publican and
the Pharisee (Luke 18:9–14), that God wants and expects the
total opposite from the Christian. The Gospel portrays the
Pharisee as self-righteous, arrogant, and proud of himself. In his

prayer, he gives a long speech to God, telling him of his accomplishments. The poor publican, however, humbles himself, and his humility pleases the Lord, and his humble prayer is therefore heard by God. The Christian is called to choose the way of the publican. It is only through true humility of heart that the monk can be liberated from the prison of his hopeless self-centeredness.

In making his the attitude of the publican, the monk is imitating the example of Christ himself, who said to all his disciples, "Learn from me, for I am gentle and humble in heart" (Matthew 11:29). From the moment of his Incarnation until the end of his life, Jesus humbled himself and became obedient even unto death (Philippians 2:7–8). Jesus is both the teacher of and the model for the monk, who can measure the validity of his life only by how close he follows the example of the Master. The monk then will hear Jesus' consoling promise to those who follow the path of humility: "You will find rest for your souls." This peace of the soul is ultimately the fruit and reward that humility brings to the monk's heart.

> The man who had come to know himself is never
> fooled into reaching for what is beyond him. He keeps
> his feet henceforth on the blessed path of humility.
> St. John Climacus, *The Ladder of Divine Ascent*

Silence

Silence is the mystery of the world to come,
Speech is the organ of this present world. . . .
Every man who delights in a multitude of words,
Even if he says admirable things, is empty within.
Silence, however, will illuminate you in God
And deliver you from the phantoms of ignorance.
Silence will unite you to God Himself.

ST. ISAAC OF NINEVEH

Silence is a very important part of all traditional monastic life. For the monk, silence creates a space where the integration of his scattered powers into a unity becomes possible. The silence of the monastery cultivates a certain atmosphere where the monk can come to the knowledge and experience of God, where he can better apprehend the mystery of his love. Silence purifies love in our hearts and strengthens and deepens our prayer. It brings light and clarity to the darkness of our minds; it gives peace and endurance to our daily work. Silence is the source of strength, harmony, and stability in the monastic day.

Exterior and interior silence are essential to the monastic life. The very nature of our style of life demands an attitude of reverence for silence. Situated in a secluded area, the monastery provides the tranquillity necessary for the development of the monk's interior life.

St. Benedict's Rule quotes Old Testament passages where the abuse of speech—too much talking—leads to sin, and he recommends strongly that it be curbed, "that permission to speak should seldom be granted even to mature disciples, no matter how good or holy or constructive their talk" (chapter 6).

St. Benedict goes beyond the simple use of silence as a repressive measure to avoid sin: he sees silence as a liberating force that frees the monk's soul to raise itself to God. In the monk who loves silence, the working of grace is given greater freedom.

Silence is observed in all monasteries in a variety of forms. There may be some insignificant differences between individual monasteries in the way silence is kept, but the essential respect for it permeates every contemplative monastery where the Rule is taken seriously. In every monastery there are "spaces of silence," where speech or conversation is not allowed. These are usually the oratory, the refectory, the dormitory and cells, the cloister, the library, and the scriptorium. The monk is taught from his very entrance into monastic life to be deferential toward the silence of others. Because of this, silence is required in all the places where the life of the community unfolds. Silence is also observed in a stricter fashion at certain times of the day: during the night (called in monasteries "the great silence," from Compline to after the completion of the morning Office), during the siesta in summer, during the hours of prayer and

Lectio, and during the meals, when reading accompanies the partaking of food.

The habit of silence among monks does not apply only to speech or conversation. Monks are encouraged to practice quiet in many practical ways, such as avoiding making noise when they walk, sit, work, close or open a door or a window. When speaking is necessary and conversations take place, monks are still quiet, subdued, and restrained—as St. Benedict encouraged.

To the extent that the monk is serious about the cultivation of silence, either in the hermitage or the monastery, the more he is filled with the tranquillity, peace, and necessary grace to apprehend the presence of God in the depths of his soul.

> These three things are appropriate for a monk: exile, poverty, and endurance in silence.
> ABBA ANDREW, *The Sayings of the Desert Fathers*

SOLITUDE

*Solitude and prayer are the greatest means to acquire
virtues. Purifying the mind, they make it possible to see
the unseen.*

*Solitude, prayer, love, and abstinence are the four
wheels of the vehicle that carries our spirit heavenward.*
ST. SERAPHIM OF SAROV

Solitude is an inner journey which not only monks but all men
and women who seek the truth must make at one time, or
preferably frequently, during their earthly lives. The difference
between those who embrace the monastic state and those who
don't is that we monks not only accept the necessity and the
validity of this journey, but we also encourage it and make time
for it.

The journey into solitude fosters a quest for our true self,
not the person that we and others think we are, but the person
that God expects us to be, made as we are in his image and likeness. Of course, this is a lifelong journey, not accomplished all at
once but requiring frequent and perhaps long sojourns into solitude. Solitude helps us face the fact that we are all, monks
included, victims of the pretensions, vanity, and illusions of a
worldly society that nurtures in us a false portrait of the self and
not the true self that God intends. Solitude is the place where we
find the grace to face the struggle between these two selves, the
false one and the true one. Solitude is also where we encounter a
God who loves us, a God who is love, life, mercy, light, and
truth and who leads us gently on the path to the discovery of
our true identity. Solitude is the place where the old, fractured

self dies and the new transformed self, helped by God's grace, emerges.

Thomas Merton, the renowned Cistercian monk and a lover of solitude, expanded on this search for the authentic self in many of his treatises. In "The Inner Experience: Christian Contemplation," he once poignantly wrote:

> I must return to Paradise.
> I must recover myself,
> salvage my dignity,
> recollect my lost wits,
> return to my true identity.

The early desert monks, with that deep realism and profound common sense that was uniquely theirs, also taught their disciples to cultivate the love of solitude. Again and again they repeated, "Stay in your cell and do not leave it. Sit in your cell, and your cell will teach you everything." For them, the humble solitude of the monastic cell was the furnace of Babylon, where the transformation from the old self into the new self in God's likeness took place. The task of the disciple was to heed his master's advice and persevere, in spite of the trials and often boredom of the cell, alone with him who is Alone. Gradually, the disciple learned to discover the wisdom of this teaching. Solitude then became for him not only the place that led to the discovery of his true identity, but it even more so became the place where he could find and work out daily his own salvation.

> In the swamp in secluded recesses,
> A shy and hidden bird is warbling a song.
> Solitary the thrush,
> The hermit withdrawn to himself, avoiding the
>   settlements,
> Sings by himself a song.
>> WALT WHITMAN, FROM
>> "WHEN LILACS LAST IN THE DOORYARD BLOOM'D"

Simplicity

*If you wish to draw the Lord to you, approach Him as
disciples to a master, in all simplicity, openly, honestly,
without duplicity, without idle curiosity. God is simple
and uncompounded, and He wants the souls that come
to Him to be simple and pure. Indeed, you will never
see simplicity separated from humility.*
ST. JOHN CLIMACUS, *The Ladder of Divine Ascent*

*True simplicity consists not in the use of particular
forms, but in foregoing overindulgence, in maintaining
humility of spirit, and in keeping the material
surroundings of our lives directly serviceable to necessary ends, even though these surroundings may properly
be characterized by grace, symmetry, and beauty.*
Book of Discipline of the Religious Society of Friends

Part of the Gospel message, as exemplified in the life of Jesus, is
an invitation to the Christian to choose true simplicity of heart,
of mind, of lifestyle. Jesus was born, lived, and died in great
simplicity, and the task of the disciple is to follow in the footsteps of the Master—for the disciple is no greater than the
Master (Matthew 10:24). As a matter of fact, true acceptance of
the Gospel, as we witness in the lives of the saints, implies a
simplified and unified existence. Christian life is truly a call to
radical simplicity.

From our daily experiences, we learn that human existence
is complex, as is the world in and around us. We are attracted to
many things at the same time, and our lives bear witness to
diverse cultural, spiritual, and biological factors. All that we are

and all that is around us seems manifold, we discover daily. We see nations at war with one another; we see ourselves as human beings at odds with one another. We feel the conflict between the body and the spirit, the tension between the mind and the heart, the rift between the individual and society at large, the strife between humankind and our environment. Complexity exists at the very core of our human existence, it is a daily fact of life, and we often are unable to handle its weight, its tensions, and its seeds of destruction.

How does the Christian monastic react to all of this? Where does he or she look for enlightenment and resolution to seemingly unsolvable tensions? The answer can only lie in the acceptance of the Gospel and its fundamental message of simplicity, based on the life and teachings of Jesus, who is the foundation rock of our faith.

As Christians, monks, and nuns, we strive for the single-mindedness of the Gospel, or what may be called simplicity of the intellect, by the complete surrender of our minds to truth. But first, filled with deep humility, we must readily acknowledge and accept the limitations of our minds and renounce all our intellectual self-presumptions and illusions. There is nothing more dangerous in a spiritual life than an attitude of vanity, superiority, and self-importance, which manifests itself in many subtle ways. Once we have renounced our self-interest and acknowledged our capacity to know and understand nothing, it is only then that our minds, enlightened by the Holy Spirit, become capable of the clear pursuit of truth for its own sake. In the process, we are given the grace to discover that truth itself is a Person, for the Lord says, "I am . . . the Truth" (John 14:6). He prays to the Father that we be rooted and consecrated in this truth (John 17:19). Grasping this truth is ever beyond the normal comprehension of our limited human minds. But God allows those who seek him with simplicity of mind and purity

of heart to discover and hold onto him who alone is truth and who deigns to show us, in his mercy, the path to life.

Authentic simplicity of heart means essentially the continual practice of self-renunciation in every life situation and turning from every form of worldly illusion. It is certainly the antithesis to the ways and wisdom of the world. "True simplicity," as the Shakers liked to call it, or "blessed simplicity," as the early Christian monks called it, helps to liberate our hearts from the worship of false idols and the exaggerated self-exaltation and glorification which is so in vogue in our day, even among so-called spiritual people. Instead, real simplicity of heart fosters within us an indescribable longing for God and his kingdom. Seek first the kingdom of God (Matthew 6:33), Jesus tells us, and this we do by giving ourselves to the task of unceasing prayer (Luke 21:36). This in turn allows us to experience the groanings of the Holy Spirit within the enclosure of our hearts, that is, at the very root of our being. This is the fulfillment of the Lord's promise when he says in the Gospel, "Blessed are the pure in heart, for they shall see God" (Matthew 5:8, RSV), for indeed simplicity of heart is nothing else than this purity of heart to which Jesus attaches the beautiful promise of the vision of God.

However, it is not possible to strive after monastic simplicity of mind and heart without also adopting a Gospel-like simple lifestyle. Following the example of the Master, monks and nuns seek to do away with all that is inessential in their everyday lives, and endeavor to live with total dependence upon God. The Christian monastic is called to renunciation of worldly cares and of attachment to earthly things and, with ever-increasing faith and passionate love for the Lord, to complete surrender to God's loving Providence. With childlike simplicity we entrust our lives, our fears, our basic need for security, and everything else to our Father's loving care. Do not "worry about your life and what you are to eat, nor about your body and what you are to wear. . . . Your heavenly Father knows you need them all" (Matthew 6:25, 33).

Monastic simplicity, thus understood, becomes a radical reaction to the false stability and security the world offers, a true beacon of hope toward attaining the blessed freedom of God's children. This simplicity directs our hearts and minds—indeed, all our actions—toward God, in whom alone the resolution and integration of our apparent complexities can be found. Monastic simplicity purifies our hearts, unifies our sense of purpose, and redirects it toward the kingdom of God. Accepted as a way of life, simplicity liberates us not only from the heavy burden of complexities but also frees us from the weight of our attachment to material, temporal things, allowing us to focus single-heartedly on Jesus, our Savior. Monastic simplicity sets us free from the violence and the conflicts found within and outside ourselves and makes us taste that a true life in Christ is peace and joy in the Holy Spirit. Finally, true Gospel simplicity brings us to the ultimate experience of the transparency of truth, the kind of truth of which Jesus spoke when he said, "I am the Way, the Truth and the Life" (John 14:6).

The older I grow, the more clearly I perceive the
dignity and the winning beauty of simplicity in
thought, conduct, and speech: a desire to simplify all
that is complicated and to treat everything with the
greatest naturalness and clarity.

POPE JOHN XXIII

In simplicity, we enter the deep silences of the heart for
which we were created.

RICHARD J. FOSTER, *Freedom of Simplicity*

God, our Maker,
Teach us to live the Gospel
In a spirit of simplicity of heart and mind.
Free us from the burden of our sins and complexities
And give us the grace to attain that unity
Which to Your own bears resemblance.

Frugality

*A frugal man should always be looking to see what he
can do without.*

Blessed Henry Suso

*Be frugal and hard-working men and women; avoid all
vanity in dress which will exclude you from heaven; try
to keep to the simplicity of manners of our forefathers
[and foremothers].*

St. Nicholas of Flue, Swiss hermit

Frugality and simplicity are cherished virtues within the
monastic tradition because they come from the teachings of the
Gospel and the example of Christ's own life. The first monks
and nuns in the desert paid heed to these attractive virtues,
leaving to the rest of us their examples and teachings as testaments.

Through the practice of voluntary frugality, we foster in
the monastery a certain attitude, a certain philosophy of life, that
is radically opposed to the values of present-day society. We view
the consumerism encouraged by governments, markets, the
media, and certain economists as totally unnecessary, wasteful,
and certainly harmful to the life of the spirit. The monk's daily
life tries to affirm the truth that we can all live better by learning
to live with less, and we deliberately assert our inner freedom by
renouncing the slavery of overconsumption.

Voluntary frugality doesn't mean necessarily living in a
state of destitution. It means learning to distinguish between the
things that we really need in daily life and those that we don't
and can do without. It means buying something because it is

needed in the monastery, not simply because we personally want it. It means treating objects, tools, and utensils with such respect that they can last more than a lifetime. It means both refusing to take part in any kind of waste and being thrifty enough to recycle most of the products discarded by our materialistic, wasteful society. Ultimately, frugality is a tool that helps us monks place our values, perspectives, and priorities on what is really important, on the one thing necessary.

Many years ago, when we needed to expand a wing of the monastery and didn't have enough material resources, someone offered us all the materials from an old house that was going to be demolished in the nearby village. With the help of a friend, we went about the task of dismantling the floors, doors, closets, windows, wood panels from the walls, and all else that could be reused in the new building. Because the wing was finally built mostly out of these recycled materials, and because some of the work—like stripping the old paint, plastering, painting—was done by ourselves, it ended up costing us less than half of what the normal cost would have been. When it came to furnishing the monastery, we have always relied on the old used furniture given to us by friends or found in the streets of New York and brought here, where we patiently repair, restore, refinish, and put them again to good use. We have a good neighbor nearby who is a professional painter, and he gives us leftover cans of paint and stains. We in turn mix the different cans until we have enough to repaint the rooms in need.

When it comes to food, we have a few chickens that provide us and our monastery guests with eggs. A garden provides vegetables during the growing season; we freeze and preserve some for the cold months. Besides the food from our gardens, one of the largest food stores in the county gives us a certain amount of vegetables and fruits that they can't sell, some of which we use to feed our animals, some of which we share with those in need, and some of which we eat ourselves. We do the same with the day-old bread and pastries that two local bakeries provide. Sometimes we even get cakes, as we did this past Christmas Eve, which we were able to serve afterward to all those who came to attend Christmas Mass.

Monastic life has always, like the Gospels, been counter-cultural. While society's incentive is to spend, expand, consume, and waste, monastics choose the opposite as a valid alternative: spend and consume less, scale back on your possessions, avoid cluttering, share and give away to others what you don't need, build small dwellings, and conserve energy and other resources. Monks deliberately make the choice of the good life instead of the trendy fast track of our times.

I think the example of monks have something to offer the world, which is largely directed to the slavery of consumption, often at the expense of the poor and the underprivileged of our planet. The monastic lessons of frugality, austerity, sobriety, and productivity have proven to be a more human, more Christ-like, and freeing alternative to the seductive, superficial view espoused by a materialistically oriented world.

> Let us learn to live simply and frugally, so that others may simply live.

The Monastic Habit

*Let the habit of the monk be such as may cover the
body and protect the monk from the cold . . . and not
such as may foster the seeds of vanity or please the fancy.
The habit should be so plain and ordinary, so that it may
not be thought remarkable for novelty of color or
fashion among other men of the same profession.*
St. John Cassian, Cenobitic Institutions

*The way the monk dresses signifies, therefore, what he is.
Much more, it partially constitutes his very monastic being.
From this fact springs the moderate but serious attention
which ancient monks constantly gave to their dress.*
Dom Adalbert de Vogüe, The Rule of St. Benedict

The monastic habit is the monk's sign of consecration to God
and a reminder to himself of having accepted a life of self-
renunciation. To embrace the monastic life, according to
St. Benedict, is to embrace a continual state of repentance and
conversion. To the monk the monastic habit is the quiet symbol
of his continual striving for conversion.

St. Benedict, having received the monastic tradition from
the East, attaches the same importance to the monastic habit as
did the early desert fathers, but he is full of common sense about
it: "The clothing to the brothers should vary according to local
conditions and climate, because more is needed in cold regions
and less in warmer. . . . We believe that for each monk a cowl
and tunic will suffice in temperate regions; in winter a woolen
cowl is necessary, in summer a thinner, lighter one, also a
scapular for work, and footwear—both sandals and shoes." Not

only is St. Benedict practical about the habit, he is also full of Gospel frugality about the way to go about obtaining the material for it. "Monks must not complain about the color or coarseness of all these articles, but use what is available in the vicinity at a reasonable cost" (Rule, chapter 55). The monk must apply the same standards of simplicity to the habit and his personal dress code as he does to other aspects of his monastic life.

In recent times there has been a tendency in some religious circles to abandon the religious habit and adopt a more secular way of dressing. After all, "the habit does not make the monk," say some of the people who promote this view. While this may be partly true, the opposite is also true, that the wearing of the habit helps make the monk. I think it is important not to confuse the adaptation made by members of active congregations to secular standards, perhaps needed because of the nature of their apostolic work, and then apply the same principles to monastic life. Religious life, as it has evolved in the Western church, and monastic life, as it has always been in both the Eastern and the Western churches, are two different entities, with very different lifestyles and distinct goals. What is of value to one is not necessarily to the other. Thus, the inner renewal demanded of each of them must proceed differently. It does a great injustice to both to try to apply exactly the same standards of renewal to both groups, when the vocations and purposes of the groups are different. Active religious orders like the Franciscans and Jesuits may find it more suited to their traditions to dress like their contemporaries (I think St. Francis would have been perfectly at home wearing a poor worker's blue jeans today). The monk, however, cannot renounce the monastic habit without sacrificing something very intrinsic to the monastic tradition. Monastic life is an organic whole, and monks don't pick and choose at random what elements in their life they should change according to the fashion of the world. The question of adapting secular standards in order to be relevant to the world should be irrelevant to the monk, for his life is meant to be a poor and humble one hidden with Christ in God, not a success story in the eyes of the world. Perhaps paradoxically, in doing this the monk can make his only claim to relevance.

The religious garment in the active orders was not necessarily a habit but a uniform, and its meaning until recently was that those wearing it belonged to a particular order or institute. Not so with the monastic habit. St. Benedict, basing his writing on the subject on the teachings of St. Basil, gives personal nuance to the value of the habit. The monk, being a weak man, needs a constant reminder of the fact of his conversion and of his resolution to lead a perfect life. The habit therefore is not a sign to help others distinguish the wearer. The value of the monastic habit is personal, it is for the monk himself; in fact, it symbolizes the soul of the monk. The monastic habit creates the visible separation between the world the monk renounces and the new life of asceticism he embraces. Moreover, the monastic habit not only reminds the monk daily of the life of conversion and repentance that he has embraced; it is also a sign of his belonging to God alone. The monastic habit, in a sense, is a symbol of the wedding garment of the Gospel, which tells the monk that he must be prepared at all times for the wedding feast, for the Bridegroom "comes as a thief in the night," and we know neither the day nor the hour. All we know is that we must wear the proper attire to be able to enter the wedding feast.

It was understood in early monasticism that the gesture by which the elder clothed the new monk with the monastic habit on the day of his profession was the sign of the transmission of a spiritual grace inherited from all the monks that preceded him.

PERE PLACIDE DESEILLE,
L'echelle de Jacob et la Vision de Dieu

The monastic habit has the twofold purpose of warning people in the world what to expect of the man who is wearing it, and of warning the man who is wearing it that he must behave in a particular way.

DOM HUBERT VAN ZELLER, *The Holy Rule*

Inner Freedom

"If you make my word your home
you will indeed be my disciples,
you will learn the truth
and the truth shall make you free"
John 8:31–32

To those who wish to achieve inner freedom, Jesus seems to demand first that they seek the truth of His word, or truth itself, for He says "I am. . . .the Truth," (John 14:6). Then this Truth will bestow on us the gift of freedom.

In order to become free, however, we must first accept the fact that we are not free. A humble, honest self-appraisal, a deep look into ourselves, will tell us that we are basically slaves— slaves of our sinfulness, habits, and vices; slaves of our prejudices and intolerance; slaves of our present culture and worldly ideas; slaves especially of the self-image we have created of ourselves, the idealized self which we portray and wish others to believe is the real us, when in fact it is not. Almost nothing is more difficult than to look at ourselves as we really are. Even more difficult yet is to accept ourselves as God ultimately accepts us. It takes a great deal of courage and honesty. That in fact is a grace.

It helps to start with the fact that Christ sees us the way we really are yet loves us. He loves us in spite of all our sinfulness, ugliness, and limitations. If Jesus accepts us and loves us such as we are, then perhaps we can begin accepting ourselves as we are and also begin to love ourselves, in spite of all, for what we indeed are.

The way to inner freedom is the way of humility and truth. We must accept ourselves as we are and others as they are with simplicity, sometimes with humor, and always with love. Love is a sign of God's presence in our lives, and it allows us to reach others beyond the narrow frame of our own selfhood.

Once we love and accept ourselves and do the same with others, we grow into the gift of inner freedom, by listening and living out Jesus' Gospel words without fear. His words, the truth, will shape every moment of our lives in such a way that we will taste in anticipation something of the joy of heaven, the supreme joy of knowing ourselves to be God's children, totally loved by Him.

> Lord, Jesus Christ
> You are the Way, the Truth, and the Life.
> Lead us through the example
> Of your life and the wisdom of your teachings
> Into the path of self-discovery
> And true acceptance of ourselves
> As we really are in Your sight.
> Help us abide by Your Word,
> The source of all truth,
> That in due time we may achieve the inner freedom
> Promised to all those who leave all things behind,
> And follow You alone until the end.

SERENITY

Detach yourself from the love of the multitude, lest your
enemy question your spirit and trouble your inner peace.
ABBA DOULAS, *The Sayings of the Desert Fathers*

Life at the threshold of the twenty-first century has become the
epitome of complexity, noise, consumerism, anxiety, and, yes,
loneliness. Perhaps one of our most difficult tasks is to cultivate
inner peace, serenity, yet all of us deeply yearn for it.

Part of the reason it is hard for us to achieve serenity and
inner freedom is that we have become accustomed to living with
the false values, rhythms, and images that our present culture
promotes. We believe we need them in our lives, when they are
totally unnecessary. How can we achieve inner peace when at
the same time we long for the company of crowds, are always in
a hurry, always have so much to do, are planning endless new
things? We thus escape the fact that we don't want to face
ourselves being alone. This sort of trend in people's everyday
lives is really a sickness, a symptom of something deeply wrong,
and the real enemy of serenity.

If we are serious about pursuing peace, one of the first
things we need to do is to bring to a halt, at least for a while, all
needless activities. We need to take time to reflect, pray, and set
goals of how to go about changing our lives. A radical change is a
must; otherwise, nothing will ever be achieved. We need to set
our priorities straight and go about organizing a life of simplicity
and centeredness, where quiet, prayer, and solitude become the
real values. We must recover or discover a real inner rhythm in
our lives and feel its liberating pulse.

We must start by first seeking or creating quiet places where we can spend a few hours a day, or one or two days a week, or a few days a month, in an ambiance that provides true grounding for the mind and the spirit. In our quest for serenity, it is important to identify, affirm, and support the inner grounding of our being. This can only be done in a space where quiet and solitude are nurtured carefully—hence the value of monasteries and retreat houses that provide this sort of haven in our midst. There it is still possible to go and hear the sounds of silence, feel the spaces of solitude, and, ultimately, enter into a state of being that makes possible a true encounter with God, the source of all serenity and peace.

In the solitude and quiet of a monastery, we discover that it is possible to achieve a life made of beauty, harmony, simplicity, and centeredness. There we may also discover that it is possible to return to the so-called real world yet let go of its glamour, anxiety, clutter, and complexity by choosing to lead a life directed toward communion with God, in whom there is neither anxiety nor complexity, but only peace, love, joy, serenity, and tranquillity. Ultimately, our life's journey becomes what we make of it, and this necessitates a choice.

> To you, O God, we turn for peace . . .
> grant us too the blessed assurance
> that nothing shall deprive us of that peace,
> neither ourselves,
> nor our foolish earthly desires,
> nor my wild longings,
> nor the anxious cravings of my heart.
> SOREN KIERKEGAARD

The Transfiguration and the Assumption: Two Glorious Summer Festivals

Having uncovered, O Savior,
a little of the light of your divinity
to those who went up with you
onto the mountain,
You have made them lovers
of your heavenly glory.
Therefore, they cried in awe:
"It is good for us to be here."
With them we also sing unto you,
O Savior Christ who was transfigured,
And say: "Let us sing unto the Lord, our God,
for he has been glorified."
BYZANTINE MATINS OF THE TRANSFIGURATION

The month of August, caught right in the heart of summer, makes all of us a bit nostalgic. It brings back memories of past summers, of lovely holidays in the country, in the mountains, or at the shore. It reminds us of the endless happy gatherings with family and friends so typical at this time, of quiet strolls through the garden and the woods, of stopping at our favorite picnic spot. Alas, there is so very much for all of us to remember!

While August brings these deep personal memories to our minds, August also brings us the joy of the two great religious festivals of the summer: the Transfiguration of the Lord on the sixth, and the glorious Assumption of Our Lady on the fifteenth.

The Transfiguration of Christ shows us the desire of the Father to glorify his Son before allowing him to undergo his Passion. For a moment, the veil is lifted up, and Jesus appears clothed in unsurpassing beauty—so luminous, so resplendent, that the disciples participating in the event can instantly recognize that it is the glory of God shining in his face. From the midst of the clouds, a voice is heard: "This is my beloved Son, with whom I am well pleased; listen to him" (Matthew 17:5, RSV). These solemn words from the Father, nearly the very words already spoken by the same voice from on high at Jesus' baptism, bear witness that Jesus is the only Son of God, true God from true God, as we profess in the Credo. With one of the Byzantine hymns for the feast, we can sing,

> Let us go up into the heavenly and holy mountain,
> Let us stand in spirit in the city of the living God,
> And let us gaze with our minds at the spiritual
>   Godhead of the Father and the Spirit,
> Shining forth in the only-begotten Son.

The mystery of the Transfiguration contains an added hidden meaning: the cosmic transformation of the world at the end of time. Another Byzantine text reads, "To show the transformation of human nature at your second and fearful coming, O Savior, you did transfigure yourself! And you have sanctified the whole universe by your light."

Human nature, which is now under the spell of sin, will be freed, renewed, when Christ comes in glory at the end of time. The light of Tabor, the light which shone from Jesus' face, sanctifies those that come close to him as the disciples did. It is also the light that nurtures our hope about the future of the world.

In the Eastern Christian tradition, the feast of the Transfiguration is also the feast of the harvest. On this day Eastern Christians keep the old custom of rendering thanks to the Lord of the harvest by bringing to the church and offering him their first vegetables, fruits, herbs, and flowers. Here in the monastery, after the Liturgy we have the traditional blessing of the produce of our garden. This is a symbol of the earth itself being made new by the presence of Christ, rendering in homage its first fruits to its Lord and Master.

The other great feast of August is dedicated to the Mother of God. On the fifteenth of August, we celebrate the Dormition, or falling asleep, of Our Lady and her Assumption into heaven. I find nothing better to describe this great mystery than to again have recourse to Byzantine texts, especially to the text sung at Vespers:

> What spiritual songs shall we now offer you, O most
>   Holy Virgin?
> For by your deathless dormition, you have sanctified
>   the whole world,
> And then you have been translated to the places above
>   the world,
> There to perceive the beauty of the Almighty
> And, as his mother, to rejoice in it exceedingly.
>
> O marvelous wonder! The source of life is laid in the
>   tomb,
> And the tomb itself becomes a ladder to heaven.
> The Bride of God, the Virgin and Queen,
> The glory of the elect, the pride of virgins,
> Is taken up to her Son.

As we celebrate these two glorious and very monastic feasts of summertime, some subtle changes begin to be noticed

in Mother Nature all around us: there are new arrivals in the garden, in the countryside, in the woods. August marks the appearance of goldenrod and loosestrife in our meadows and ponds, and the sound of the cricket rings stridently in our ears during the long, warm evenings. Among the August arrivals that one becomes very fond of throughout the years are the delicious blackberries, by this time well ripened, peaches, plums, and early melons. Of course, the wonderful new corn is plentiful at this time.

With the arrival of August, we reach the peak of our seasonal garden work. Though it is hard and laborious, one feels deeply enriched by it. Our gardens have grown quite extensive throughout the years, and it is a full-time job to care for them. In the perennial garden, there is always something in bloom from early spring until late November. The other gardens are a mixture of annuals, biennials, perennials, and wildflowers. They fill the corners and borders with charming colors and delightful fragrances. One needs only to step outdoors to perceive the sweet scent arising from the beds of lilies, roses, and flowering Nicotiana. Likewise, on the left hand side of the chapel, as one walks into the herb garden, one nearly becomes inebriated with the strong aroma that arises from the herbs: lavender, mints, rosemary, thyme, and lemon verbena. This is particularly true in the early morning or early evening, or simply just after a rain.

Summer is an extraordinary season. It brings subtle changes in nature and calls forth growth and transformation on all of us. The lush exuberance and intensity of summer living has a profound influence on our human experience: our innermost thoughts, our intuitions, our interactions with others, our relationships with our own selves and with God. Summer gives us a vivid sense of the reality of living and instigates the continuous discovery of what living is for. When the summer days begin to wane in the monastery and the summer moon drifts away, we are ready to move forward into the next cycle, the quiet ripening of the seeds planted by the Holy Spirit in the soil of our lives.

> These long, quiet summer days, I have been much alone. The cicadas rasp the still air; the birds are silent now, and in the near woods the squirrels are clipping down the unripe nuts from the hickory trees. It is the still middle age of the year: the time of sunny fullness, of harvest, of fulfillment. . . . It seems to me I want now to be quiet for a century or so to consider all the things I have ever seen and heard and felt and thought. It is not the multiplication of our seeing that increases our lives, but the penetration of them.
> DAVID GRAYSON, *The Countryman's Year,* AUGUST

Autumn

Work in
Monastic Life

The Work of Love

My dear friends,
let us love each other,
since love is from God
and everyone who loves is a child of God and knows God.
Whoever fails to love does not know God,
because God is love.

1 John 4:7-8

Love's birthplace is God. There it is born, there it is
nourished, there it is reared. There it is at home, not a
tourist, but a native. For by God alone is love given,
and in him it endures.
William of St. Thierry, *The Nature and Dignity of Love*

An early monk once described the purpose of monastic life as
"to cling to that most excellent way which is love." To truly
follow in the footsteps of Christ, the monk has to learn to walk
the way of love. And the way of love of the Gospels is not easy.
It is full of pitfalls. Love is not obtained by simply wanting it,
nor is it something we gain merely by willing it. Love is something we work at every day.

The dynamic work of love is the center of monastic life.
The heart of the monk, touched by grace, is able to see the
painful reality of his brokenness and sinfulness, and at the same
time encounter the tenderness and loving mercy of a God who
alone can forgive him and free him from his own pitfalls. The
deep realization of this personal, all-powerful love of God for
the least of his creatures is the dynamic that starts the monk on
his monastic journey and that pushes him forward toward its

fulfillment. Enveloped as he is by God's love, the monk discovers that to imitate God and follow his ways implies choosing to do the work of love. To become loving and compassionate to all his brothers and sisters and to all created things, as Jesus was, is then his only goal.

This goal, however, is not easily attainable, for the monk, in his poverty, is continually confronted by his limitations. Daily he must begin again and again the work of love. In trying to do the work of love, the monk must not put his trust in his own strength or his own resources. In the midst of the struggle, he must call upon the Holy Spirit, the Spirit of love, to take over and lead the work to completion. He must rely on God alone.

Christ showed us the way of love, and he practiced it to the end by his self-emptying on the Cross. The monk, in imitation of his master, is called to put love into practice by means of self-renunciation and by embracing the Cross of Christ. According to the monastic tradition, the monk does this concretely by the living out of his monastic profession. By accepting obedience, the monk renounces his own personal will and chooses instead to do only the will of God. By accepting conversion of life, which encompasses the poverty and chastity that are part and parcel of all monastic life, the monk lays aside his claims to ownership and possessions and renounces the blessing of sexual union and fruitfulness. By accepting stability in the monastery, the monk renounces mobility and his independence. Thus, the vows of the monastic life, by which the monk slowly learns to renounce himself and to cleave to God alone, becomes the most pure expression of his love for the Lord.

The work of love is extended and expressed in the daily practice of charity toward the brethren. For the Christian the love of God and the love of neighbor cannot be separated. People dwelling either inside or outside the monastery are real to the monk, for God has stamped in each person his image and likeness. The monk understands this, so he tries not to exclude anyone, neither the stranger nor even his enemies, from the task of loving them. The work of love is absolutely real, the true meaning of the monk's existence; it absorbs him wholly.

In chapter 53 of the Rule, St. Benedict mentions quite matter-of-factly that "all guests who arrive at the monastery should be received as Christ, because he will say, 'I was a stranger, and you took me in.' . . . When a guest is announced, the monks should greet him with charity . . . for in the person of the guest, it is Christ who is really being received." St. Benedict goes on to say that "special care be taken of the poor and pilgrims, for in them especially is Christ received." The work of monastic hospitality is very much a part of the work of love which is the monk's life's task. Hospitality provides a concrete way for the monk to exercise the work of love with persons who live outside the monastery. This is at times a real challenge, but so that there may not remain the slightest doubt about this in the monk's mind, St. Benedict has assured him that he is showing charity to Christ himself.

> Love is not in the first place a sentiment, but a definite work which gets more and more exciting, the further one goes; and then from there any "activities" take on their true proportions, they are not so important.

> The work of love is to see the center [God] in others as their one reality, and then of loving the person in his reality.
>
> MOTHER MARIA, *Her Life in Letters*

The Work of Hospitality

All guests who present themselves are to be welcomed
as Christ, for he himself will say: "I was a stranger and
you welcomed me." Proper honor must be shown to all,
especially those who share our faith and to pilgrims.
Rule of St. Benedict, CHAPTER 53

Through the ancient practice of hospitality, monks share their
life with their fellow men. According to the Benedictine tradition, the doors of the monastery are open to all who come
seeking the peace of God, without distinction of belief or background. For the guests the prayer, the silence, and the warm,
fraternal welcome makes the monastery a real oasis of peace.

Monastic hospitality is different from other forms of
hospitality, because it is primarily inspired by faith, not by
protocol or any other worldly motive. It is marked by the
warmth of Christian love and the simplicity of the Gospel.
St. Benedict counsels the monks to receive guests, who represent

Christ, with "a bow of the head or by a complete prostration of the body, because Christ is indeed welcome in them" (Rule, chapter 53).

Monasteries humbly open the doors of their guesthouses to persons of good will who come seeking the peace of God, the *pax* which remains the ideal of every Benedictine monastery. The guests may come alone or in small groups, and they are asked by the monks to respect the contemplative atmosphere of the monastery and its daily schedule. Since prayer and work are the principal activities of all monasteries, the guests are invited to participate in them and to bring their own contributions to the tasks.

Located far from the crowds of the cities and distant enough from noisy roads, a monastery offers its guests

> a place of rest and quiet
> a space of silence
> an atmosphere of warmth and simplicity
> a house of prayer
>   where the guests can participate
>   in the rhythms of the monastic life
> and find time to listen to the Word of God
>   in the solitude of their hearts.

A brother came to a certain solitary, and when he was going away from him, he said, "Forgive me, Father, for I have made you break your rule." The solitary in turn replied, "My rule is to receive you with hospitality and to send you away in peace."

H. WADDELL, *The Desert Fathers*

The Work of Prayer

*I think there is no labor greater than that of prayer to
God. For every time a man wants to pray, his enemies,
the demons, want to prevent him, for they know that it
is only by turning him from prayer that they can hinder
his journey. Whatever good work a man undertakes, if
he perseveres in it, he will attain rest. But prayer is
warfare to the last breath.*
> Abba Agathon, *The Sayings of the Desert Fathers*

*After a long spell of prayer, do not say that nothing has
been gained, for you have already achieved something.
For, after all, what higher good is there than to cling to
the Lord and to persevere in unceasing union with Him?*
> St. John Climacus, *The Ladder of Divine Ascent*

Prayer is the inner symphony in the life of the monk. Prayer is
the one purpose, the aim toward which all his strength and
efforts are directed. According to St. Benedict, a man who enters
a monastery does it primarily with the intention of seeking God.
Everything else is secondary to this, subordinated to this end.
How does the monk seek God; how does he look for him in this
life? How is this life expressed? Like all Christians, the monk
has first received the gift of faith. He is rooted in it, and it is ultimately faith that evokes and nurtures his total response to God.
Faith tells him that God is not just an abstract idea or an ethereal
being, but a living God in whose presence he stands.

The fact that God became human is the great mystery of
Christianity, for God became human that humankind might
become God. This speaks of the unfathomable love and care of

God for his creatures. We humans have become partakers of the nature of God, as St. Peter tells us, by being raised to the dignity of "divine sonship" by adoption. God, in his love, has created the possibility for people to relate to him in a new way. God pours his Holy Spirit into every human being, and it is by this Spirit that we are able to say, "Abba, Father."

In the light of this new relationship to God, one can explain the life of the monk, for he understands this relation of sonship to the Father and hears in the depths of his heart the divine invitation to live solely for God and with him. "Come," God says, "I am Life." The monk's life then becomes a natural unfolding of this new, intimate friendship with God. This relationship finds its expression in the life of prayer, which expresses best the totality of this involvement of humans with God. It is natural therefore that the whole life of the Christian monk should gravitate toward prayer, toward living in close, conscious union with God.

To understand this even more clearly, we must look at what the Sacred Scriptures say about prayer, for the Word of God is the daily bread of the monk. St. Paul, in his first letter to the Thessalonians, counsels all Christians to "pray without ceasing." The monk, who is simply an ordinary Christian, takes this counsel to heart and makes of it the very reason for his life. Prayer becomes the very center and source of his being, the perspective from which he looks at all things, the end toward which his whole life tends. Following the invitation of the Divine Master, "Go to your room, close your door, and pray to your Father in private" (Matthew 6:6, NAB), the monk's life is marked by this continual journey into the depths of his heart to seek the face of God. This is perhaps the chief characteristic distinguishing the monastic life from other forms of Christian life: the intensity of the monk's interior journey and the profundity from which he is called to pray.

Prayer opens our hearts to the reality of God and others. For the monk, God and humankind are not two separate concerns but very much one, the one being part of the other. Instead of dichotomizing, prayer brings all things into unity, helping one see the underlying interrelation of all things. In the light of God, one comes to see all things as one. Prayer when perfected by grace, leads one to recognize the presence of Christ in every human being.

Although prayer is the daily occupation of the monk, it is by no means easy for him—nor is it for any other Christian, for that matter. It is true that at times one can experience deep joy and peace in prayer, but it is also true that prayer is often a struggle. One does not always find oneself ready to pray. Even in a monastery, there are the daily worries, vicissitudes, and distractions of ordinary living; these at times seem to be obstacles to real prayer. One often feels lazy, bored, and almost incapable of going down into one's heart to pray. Tediousness can create resistance to some forms of ascetic discipline, which must accompany all striving for prayer.

Then there is that which is perhaps the most difficult of all: the need to face oneself as one is before God. This, more than anything else, discourages people from prayer. It is even more difficult to know that after having acknowledged what one is, one has to do something about it.

Prayer is rooted in the experience of daily life. Monks have to face the same difficulties that others do in trying to pray. This struggle is daily. At the same time, monastics realize that the "kingdom of heaven suffers violence," that it is natural that one should struggle to possess it. Monks and other Christians have heard Christ saying to his disciples that one must "watch and pray" so as not to fall into the subtle traps of the Evil One. Very often, just like their predecessors the desert fathers, monks have to confront the Evil One in many faces. They are then

reminded of the truth of Christ's words that there are "certain demons that can be conquered only by fasting and prayer."

All Christian life is a call to conversion, to *metanoia,* to the rebirth and blossoming of the new person in Christ. This, of course, does not happen immediately. It is an ongoing process, something that should be happening every day of our lives. It is here that monks do a service to the Church and to society at large: we remind others of these fundamental values and of our calling to total conversion in order to partake of the divine life and thus become new beings in Christ. Christianity makes sense only in the light of this possible transformation. In the busyness of everyday living, it is easy to forget the fundamental aims and direction of all Christian living. Monks, by trying to live a very ordinary life of fidelity and prayer, of simplicity and work, of discipline, silence, and hospitality, strive to work out this process of conversion and, moved by the Holy Spirit, orient the totality of our human existence toward God, the One Absolute. Monks remember daily the "narrow way" of the Gospel, conscious that this leads one to the final transformation in Christ.

However, in doing this, we are conscious that all Christians are called to the same end in one way or another. The Gospel of Christ is not addressed only to monks or to any other particular group, but equally to all people without distinction. In a sense, there is no such thing as a monastic spirituality, but only a Christian spirituality derived directly from the teachings of the Gospel. Monks, by taking to heart the counsel of the Gospel, by giving ourselves seriously to a life of prayer, seeking only the "one thing necessary," do the service of reminding all our fellow human beings of the essence of the Christian life.

> That prayer has great power
> Which a person makes with all his might.
> It makes a sour heart sweet,
> A sad heart merry,
> A poor heart rich,
> A foolish heart wise,
> A timid heart brave,
> A sick heart well,
> A blind heart full of sight,
> A cold heart ardent.
> It draws down the great God into the little heart,
> It drives the hungry soul up into the fullness of God.
> It brings together two lovers,
> God and the soul,
> In a wondrous place where they speak much of love.
> MECHTHILDE OF MAGDEBURG, THIRTEENTH-CENTURY BEGUINE

THE WORK OF GOD:
PSALMODY

The true monk should have prayer and psalmody
continually in his heart.
    ABBA EPIPHANIUS, *The Sayings of the Desert Fathers*

The Psalms are the true garden of the solitary and the
scriptures are his paradise.
    THOMAS MERTON, *Thoughts in Solitude*

The Psalter, as the Book of Psalms is commonly called by
monks, is a place where God and the monk meet daily. Through
praying the words of the psalms, the monk shares in the experience of the chosen people of the Bible, for whom the psalms
were their daily prayers. In the psalms the monk hears the
supplications of the people of God; their cries of fear, anguish,
and suffering; their expressions of joy, praise, and thanksgiving;
and even at times the cries of desperation, resentment, and revolt
against God. All human experience is found and expressed
somewhere in the psalms.

    The Psalms, more than any other book of prayers,
expresses the interaction between God and humanity that has
been going on from the first moments of creation. For the
monk, to pray the psalms means to enter into this dialogue
through history. This history reveals to us God's actions in the
midst and on behalf of his people. God creates man and woman;
he calls them to a life of union with him. When they disobey
him, God throws them out of paradise, but he promises them a
Redeemer. In the meantime, God watches over his people and

enters into an alliance with them, an alliance that ultimately finds its fulfillment with the arrival of the promised Savior.

All this and more is expressed and prayed in the psalms. This divine reality, revealed and encountered there, becomes for the monk the manna from above that daily nourishes his inner life. Through the psalms the monk expresses to God not only the totality of his own sentiments, but that of the whole of humanity. The psalms are for the monk a cry to God for liberation on behalf of all people.

St. Benedict arranged the daily monastic schedule around the Work of God, which he considered the chief occupation of the monk. The Work of God—or the Divine Office, as it was later called—consisted of eight periods of formal prayer distributed throughout the day, of which the psalms were the main component. Besides the psalms there also were hymns, readings, responses, and other prayers, but psalmody, the singing of the psalms, constituted the principal part of the Work of God. The daily psalm singing as praise of God played a central role for St. Benedict and the early monks not so much as a method of prayer but as a true experience of God in prayer. Psalmody, said Thomas Merton, "brings us in direct contact with Him whom we seek." Psalmody, in other words, was the ordinary means for the monk to approach the presence of the living God. Thus, St. Benedict admonishes the monk that "nothing must be preferred or take precedence to the Work of God."

The ancient monks used to sing the 150 psalms in one day, sometimes several times in one day. St. Benedict, with his usual sense of balance and moderation, distributed the 150 psalms throughout the space of a week. St. Benedict also distributed the order of the psalms according to the characters of the different hours of the day and the rhythm of the seasons, especially the liturgical seasons. The first Office of the day was the night Office now called Vigils, celebrated in the time of St. Benedict around 2:00 A.M. Today some monasteries and individual monks

still retain the night character of this Office. Others celebrate it late at night before retiring to bed, and others in the very early hours of the morning at rising. The Office of Lauds follows, in which the psalms and canticles of praise are sung, which is why this Office is sometimes called Morning Praise.

The little hours—the Offices of Prime, Terce, Sext, and None—were recited during the first, third, sixth, and ninth hours of the day. These hours corresponded approximately to our present 6:00 A.M., 9:00 A.M., noon, and 3:00 P.M., depending on the particular season of the year. Today Prime has been suppressed in most monasteries because it is simply a duplication of the more important hour of Lauds. In some monasteries, following the liturgical adaptations of the Church after the last Ecumenical Council, keep only one little hour, which is usually celebrated at noon and is called the Noonday Office.

The hour of Vespers, considered by some the most solemn Office of the day, was celebrated at sunset and the rising of the evening star. Vespers, one of the most beautiful Offices of the monastic day, originated in the tradition of Jewish synagogue worship, which was adapted and continued by the early Christians and monks of the primitive Church. Psalm 140, speaking of the "evening sacrifice," is considered the official psalm of Vespers. Besides Psalm 140 and various other psalms, the "Phos Hilaron," a second-century hymn to Christ, is sung every day in our monastery. This beautiful hymn refers to Christ as the "evening light." The Office concludes with the Magnificat, Mary's song of praise to God for his goodness and wonders. The last Office of the monastic day, Compline, is celebrated at day's end just before retiring, while darkness covers the earth. The psalms of Compline are the same every day: Psalms 4, 90, and 133. With the proper hymn of the hour, they quite appropriately constitute the night prayer of the monk.

The psalms, as they were in the synagogue and in the early Church, are always sung, whether in monasteries by the monastic community or in the hermitage by the monk alone. The psalms were composed to be sung in praise of God, and they convey their true meaning only when they are sung. It is not always as important how beautifully they are sung as how prayerfully and fervently.

As the days and months and years of the life of the monk pass and are shaped ever more deeply by the worship of God through the daily chanting of the psalms, he comes to realize in his innermost being the truth of the words of the psalmist:

> How lovely is your dwelling place,
> Lord, God of hosts. . . .
> They are indeed blessed,
> those who dwell in your house
> forever singing your praise.
>   Psalm 84: 1, 4, sung version

> The Divine Office is at the same time the word of God for man and the work of man for God. It is God's revelation of himself in human accents, it is man's debt repaid to him in the medium of sacrifice.
>   Dom Hubert Van Zeller, *The Holy Rule*

The Work and Sound of Praise: The Chant

*When you sing with your voice, a moment comes when
you stop singing; then it is the moment to begin singing
with your life, and you will never stop singing.*
ST. AUGUSTINE

Beautiful sound reinforces the power of beautiful words.
G. VAN DER LEEUW, *Sacred and Profane Beauty*

The worship of God, the principal occupation of the monk, is
accomplished daily in the celebration of the Divine Office and
the Eucharist. This worship of God, in the thought of St.
Benedict, should be performed by the monk with the reverence,
respect, and beauty that is owed to God. St. Benedict cites Psalm
138, "In the presence of angels I sing to you," then says to the
monk, "Let us consider, then, how we ought to behave in the
presence of God and his angels, and let us stand to sing the
psalms in such a way that our minds are in harmony with our
voices."

The monastic chant, in particular the Gregorian chant,
which is perhaps the best expression of the monastic chant in the
West, plays an important role in enhancing the monk's worship
of God. In the words of an expert, Dom Gajard, the famous
choirmaster of the Abbey of Solesmes: "the chant is both prayer
and liturgy; it is the liturgical prayer celebrated in song." The
function of the chant in the Liturgy is to be a vehicle of prayer, a
vehicle that raises the monk's soul to express the praise of God
in the most beautiful way possible.

Dó-mi-nus di- xit ad me: Fí- li- us mé-us es tu, e-go hó- di- e gé-nu- i te.

The Gregorian chant, because of its simplicity and beauty, has served well throughout the centuries as monks' normal tool of enhancing the worship of God in the Liturgy. First of all, it is important to notice that there is an intrinsic unity between the notes of the chant and the text of the Liturgy. Sound and words are intimately connected in Gregorian chant; one cannot exist without the other. The words give meaning to the music and convert the chant into a song that prays. As Dom Gajard used to say, "Gregorian chant above all things is prayer, and nothing but prayer. It is sung and directed to God alone."

The Gregorian repertoire is so ancient and vast that it provides the diversity of expression required by the various liturgical seasons and feast days of the Church year. For instance, the Gregorian repertoire of Advent and Christmas is very different from that of Lent and Easter, and these two are also different from that which is now called the "ordinary time." The chant grew up in the Latin Church throughout the centuries, and it was particularly cultivated in monasteries as the most fitting form of worship and praise. There are various traditions of chants, depending on their places of origin: the Roman chant, the Mozarabic chant from Spain, the Ambrosian chant from Milan, the Sarum chant from England, and of course the Gregorian chant, the best known of all of them, which has survived up to our own time.

The melodies of the Gregorian chants are written according to modes, not in the traditional tonal music known to us today. Consequently, the chants contain a colorful, expressive character all their own. There are eight modes in the Gregorian chant, each with a particular flavor, which provide for this wonderful variety of expression, color, and character. The Gregorian chant is also different from other music by the fact that it has no tempo, only rhythm. In many ways the subtly modal character of the free-rhythm chant makes the Gregorian chant so perfectly apt as the sung expression of prayer. It is a form of music whose very structure is geared to prayer and leads to contemplation. In comparison to other church music, the purity of Gregorian melody is such that besides articulating the richness of the liturgical text, it creates a serene climate that allows the monk's soul to be raised tranquilly and naturally up to the heights of contemplation, deep into the mystery of God.

> That which happens in Liturgy is impossible without music, without poetry, without gesture, without emotion. There a man is brought to that which is true. He should be gratified in his arms, legs, eyes, ears, head, and heart: he should rise, genuflect, sing, listen, close his eyes, join hands, be silent. . . . Pity the man who must do all this without music because he has unlearned how to sing . . . without gesture because he has forgotten he has a body . . . without a festive air because he no longer likes to adorn.
> BERNARD HUYBERS, *The Performing Audience*

The Work of Sacred Reading: Lectio Divina

So, as Christians, having learnt from the holy Scriptures and from holy revelations, let us know the great goodness of God for those who sincerely take refuge in him and who correct their past faults by repentance, and let us not despair of our salvation.
    Abba Paul the Simple, *The Sayings of the Desert Fathers*

The high esteem in which the words of Scripture were held by the monks as well as the frequent recommendations to memorize and recite the sacred texts suggest the presence within desert monasticism of a culture nourished in significant ways on the Scriptures. Besides its place in the public sinaxis, Scripture also played a key part in the life of the cells, where it was recited, ruminated, and meditated upon both in small groups of monks and by individuals in solitude.
    D. Burton-Christie, *The Word in the Desert*

To the monk who comes to the monastery with the exclusive purpose of seeking God, St. Benedict offers different activities that will encourage him in his search. One thoroughly monastic activity, deeply rooted in the tradition, is what is commonly called in monasteries Lectio Divina, the reflective, prayerful pondering on the word of God in the Sacred Scriptures. The monk, moved by the Holy Spirit and encouraged by the Rule, takes time out daily to immerse himself, through prayerful reading, in this living contact with the Word of God. During this blessed, quiet time of sacred reading, the Holy Spirit takes over. Little by little, in an almost imperceptible way, the Spirit develops in the monk an increasing taste for the Word of God and for all things concerning a life of union with God.

The Sacred Scriptures then become not just one book among many but, indeed, a very special book. For the monk, as for all Christians, it is not only the book that contains the revealed Word of God, it is the book that *is* the Word of God. To the monk who, in the silence of his heart, learns to listen to this Word with both humility and wonder, the Word feeds him mysteriously with the knowledge of God. It encourages him, comforts him, and enlightens him as he tries to make progress in his monastic life. The Word of God as found in the Scriptures is indeed the daily bread of the monk, for it reveals the depths of God's ineffable mystery, a mystery hidden from all eternity.

Ordinarily, every monastery designates a portion of the day to the practice of Lectio Divina. In many monasteries, this activity usually takes place in the early morning after the Offices. Later on in the afternoon or evening, especially at the end of the day, the monk tries to find time to return again to sacred reading, to quiet repose in the presence of him whom his heart loves and longs for. The place where the monk usually engages in Lectio Divina is his monastic cell, where he dwells alone with God. Consequently, because of the divine interaction that takes place there, little by little the cell of the monk becomes transformed into a living furnace, where the fire of the Holy Spirit shines brightly day and night.

Although the primary objective of Lectio Divina is the reading, meditating, and praying over the Sacred Scriptures, reading other spiritual texts such as those of the fathers of the Church, the early fathers and mothers of monasticism, the texts of the liturgy, and books on prayer, are also permitted during the time assigned to Lectio. After all, these books are directly inspired by the Scriptures, and, ultimately, by the Holy Spirit, who cannot be limited to the Scriptures alone for the Spirit indeed breathes where he wills. During the time spent and allotted to Lectio, the monk's main concern should be using this time wisely to encounter the living God who wishes to speak and reveal himself to the monk's heart. The time of Lectio Divina is time for God alone, and anything else that may interfere with, interrupt, or distract the monk from this one purpose is simply completely out of place. With deep humility, the monk ought to pray to the Holy Spirit daily to guide him in wisely organizing his time of Lectio Divina, so that this truly becomes a time of spiritual rest, of intense, intimate prayer, and of authentic contemplative peace, that allows the monk to leisurely bask in God's presence.

> When the monk reads, let him seek for savor and not for science. Holy Scripture is the well of Jacob from which the waters are drawn which will be poured out later in prayer. Thus there will be no need to go to the oratory to begin to pray; but in reading itself, means will be found for prayer and contemplation.
> ABBOT ARNOUL OF BOHERISS, *Speculum Monachorum*

THE WORK OF OUR HANDS

*We do urge you, brothers, to go on making even greater
progress and to make a point of living quietly, attending
to your own business and earning your living, just as we
told you to, so that you are seen to be respectable by
those outside the Church, though you do not have to
depend on them.*

1 THESSALONIANS 4:10–12

*When they live by the labor of their hands, as our
fathers and the apostles did, then they are truly monks.*

The Rule of St. Benedict, CHAPTER 48

The early monks and nuns supported themselves by the work of
their hands, usually weaving mats, hats, rugs, and baskets, which
they later sold in the nearby local markets. Following the
example and teachings of the apostles, the early monks and nuns
seriously applied themselves to the humble task of earning their
living, not wishing to be burdens to anyone. St. Benedict, deeply
rooted as he was in the early monastic tradition, handed down
the same teaching to his monks. He observes in the Rule that at
certain hours of the day, the monk must be engaged in work,
manual or otherwise, according to the needs of the monastery,
and thus contribute to its support.

Work is an integral part of all human life, be it inside or
outside a monastery. What perhaps differentiates the monk's
approach to work from that of his fellow humans is the attitude
he brings to it. Monastery work is functional. It is not motivated
by a desire for a career or for success, or even less by greed. The
function of monastic work first of all consists in the imitation of

Jesus, the humble carpenter of Nazareth, who came to give us the example of how to live and order our lives. The second function of monastic work is to provide for the needs of the monastery and to help support the monastic community. The third function of monastic work—and this is overlooked by some—is the element of balance which work brings to the daily rhythm of the monastic life. The monk's day-to-day routine consists of trying to strike a balance between prayer and work, reading, study, and rest. This balance is essential, for it contributes to freeing the monk's mind and heart for the purpose for which he came to the monastery, that is, communion with God. Monastic work, though done in the solitude and enclosure of a monastery, adds another positive, redemptive dimension to the life of the monk. Through it the monk is permitted to share in the suffering, hardness, and insecurities of workers all around the world. It allows him to express his solidarity with all those who also must earn their daily bread "with the sweat of their brows."

The concrete aspects of monastery work are many. The work depends on the practical needs of the place and the community, the commands of obedience, and the particular talents of the individual monk. First of all, there is the general maintenance of the monastic buildings and property. Then there is the cleaning and other regular work of the various departments of a monastery: the chapel, sacristy, library, refectory, kitchen, laundry, and guesthouse. There is also the heavy manual labor required on the farm, in the gardens, for wood-splitting, and with other outdoor chores. The particular industry of each monastery, the product of the monks' hands—foods, icons, and more—is marketed to support the monastery. Then there are offices and tasks assigned to individual monks, such as porter, guestmaster, cellarer, archivist, librarian, cook, carpenter, electrician, infirmarian, and other roles similar to those of any ordinary household.

The work of our small farm and gardens is an ever-engaging task. Farming may not always be very remunerative, but I have found that it is one of the instruments that keeps us monks grounded in reality, making us grow daily in the awareness of our total dependence on God. For this reason, monks usually choose to live close to the soil—and thus to the God who makes it fertile. Here at Our Lady of the Resurrection, we now raise only sheep and a few chickens, which provide us with eggs for the table year 'round. Cultivating our gardens is equally demanding work, but a bit more remunerative, since it provides food for the table and products to sell weekly at the local farmer's market in Millbrook.

Like other local farmers, our monastery has a small stand at the market where we sell the products from our farm and gardens: eggs, dips, herbal vinegars, jams and marmalades, honey, chutneys and sauces, relishes and pickles, dried culinary herbs, and a variety of prepared food. This weekly market experience is a rather humble and sober one, and follows the tradition of the early desert monks and nuns. And this experience provides me also a better understanding of chapter 5 of the Rule, where St. Benedict counsels monks to avoid greed in pricing and to sell their wares a little bit lower than people outside the monastery, so that in all things God may be glorified. This is not always simple or easy; it demands a certain amount of discretion and discernment, virtues greatly encouraged by the Rule.

But besides reinforcing virtues of the Rule, the weekly market experience is deeply satisfying in that it allows a monk to share the same tensions, frustrations, hard work, joys, and rewards of the other local farmers. This creates a certain solidarity between all of us. When I first began offering our monastery wares there were many who blinked in disbelief— they didn't know what to make of a monk's presence in their midst. Today, however, the other salespeople have bonded in friendship with me, understanding better that we monks share the same uncertainty and struggles in trying to earn an income with the work of our hands. The level of acceptance is such that at times some of them approach me to exchange some of their produce with me according to our mutual needs or confide a problem and then ask me to pray for them.

Work is an inescapable feature of daily monastic living. A good monk does not seek to avoid it; instead, he approaches it with a humility that fosters a prayerful attitude to permeate his work. He lets the joys and sufferings experienced during work time find places in his daily prayer, so that, as St. Benedict counsels in the Rule, "God may be glorified in all things."

> Go to a monastery expecting to see other worldly men and women, and you will be disappointed and possibly scandalized by the time spent there in such mundane tasks as milking cows, manuring fields, pitching hay, baking bread, keeping bees, making jelly. Yet the secret of holiness, wholeness, and health is there, for the life is a carefully, even artistically, constructed dialogue of the spirit with creation. Out of that dialogue grows true humanness.
>
> JAMES DESCHENE, "THE MYSTIC AND THE MONK: HOLINESS AND WHOLENESS"

A Simple Space for God

The Lord's house is built on the top of the mountain, it
is high above the hills. From the ends of the earth men
come running to it, crying out, "Glory to You, Lord!"
                                        Isaiah 2:2–3

In 1977, after several years of pilgrimage in properties belonging
to other religious communities, after struggling and waiting for a
more permanent home, the Lord provided us with the property
where our monastery stands today. It stands on a rural hilltop in
Dutchess County, properly secluded. Our enclosure consists of
twenty-two acres and originally contained two small bungalows
distant from each other. One of these bungalows—renovated and
partitioned into four bedrooms, a lavatory, kitchen facilities, and
a small eating area—became our St. Scholastica Guesthouse. This
small, frugal building is where we accommodate guests, who, as
St. Benedict points out, are never lacking in a monastery. The
other bungalow, named for St. Benedict, became the nucleus for
the monastery.

Throughout the years, we have made small additions to
this nucleus, creating more space for a library, workroom, and
other useful rooms. There is nothing superfluous in our modest
buildings or on our property, and all the added construction was
done in a style of rustic simplicity. After several years here, our
last undertaking was building the monastic church as a true
house of prayer. Built on the summit of a high hill, this church
stands visibly as a pointer to God and a sign of hope for all who
come here to pray.

The architecture of our small church is simple and in an
accessible scale, combining both Old World and New World

tradition—that is, our ancient roots and those of our new home. The building is a marriage of wood and stone found here in Dutchess County—materials used in Dutchess' early and contemporary architecture. The church thus is a concrete sign of the mystery of the Incarnation in our midst.

Worship, where the monastery draws its quiet and steady pulse, takes place four times a day in this church. We sing Vigil and Lauds in the early morning stillness and a small Hour at noon (a welcome relief in the middle of the day). Vespers follows at dusk: we offer this evening song of prayer and thanksgiving to God for the gift of light. Our final prayer, Compline, closes the monastic day at nighttime. The Gregorian and ancient Russian monastic chants that we use daily in our worship seem to harmonize perfectly with the austere lines and contours of our small church, making us realize deeply that this simple place is a space for God, a space where the living God lays down his tent among his people.

> A monastery, it seems to me, speaks to the people of our times because it portrays a balance, an equilibrium, a harmony which is the result of the blending of different aspects of our life: our prayer and chant manifests a true desire for God, our simple life and manual work keep us in touch with all earthly realities, our fraternal relations have a quality and intensity of their own, always respecting the individuality of the person; then, through opening the doors to our guests in welcome, we symbolically open the doors of the monastery to the world, to everything that is human and good in it.
>
> REFLECTIONS OF A FRENCH MONK ON THE 1500TH
> ANNIVERSARY OF THE BIRTH OF ST. BENEDICT

Feasts of the Harvest

Come, ye thankful people, come;
Raise the song of harvest home:
All is safely gathered in
Ere the winter's storms begin.
God, our Maker, doth provide
For our wants to be supplied;
Come to God's own temple, come,
Raise the song of harvest home.
HENRY ALFORD (1810–1871), THANKSGIVING HYMN

In the monastery, where the rhythms of the Liturgy are deeply intertwined with the rhythm of the seasons, the arrival of the autumn months signals the end of the agricultural year. During September, and even more during October and November, the last of the rich crops are harvested and stored for winter use, freeing the land for a period of rest until the next spring comes around.

In early October it is a beautiful sight to behold the wheat and corn standing tall under a blue, cloudless sky in the nearby fields of the local farms. The gently rolling farmland of Dutchess County and neighboring Litchfield County in Connecticut—with their stone-fenced fields covered with pumpkins, squash, potatoes, and the last of the ripe tomatoes—is indeed a sight to behold. To this I must add another sight, quite prevalent in this region: apple orchards covered with fruit and vineyards with pale and purple grapes lined in heavy clusters coming to full fruition and extending their sweet, ripe aroma to all those who approach close. During our early autumn months when the weather is perfect, our eyes truly feast on a banquet of beauty in

the surrounding countryside: a tapestry of harvest fields, orchards and vineyards in the meadows, the glory of the maple trees in full color, the bright sunlight, and the crystal-clear, intoxicating fall air!

In monasteries, as in other farms and households, there is a heavy round of activities related to the harvest and preparations for the upcoming winter. It is the time to consolidate the summer's gains and process the earth's produce in manifold ways. There are bushels of new potatoes, all sorts of squashes, onions, garlic, and apples to be stored away safely in the monastery cellar for winter consumption. There are the endless amounts of freezing, canning, preserving, jam- and jelly-making out of the fruits of the harvest. These are all time-consuming activities, but necessary to those of us who make an effort to live from the work and products of the land. There are also the harvesting and drying of the kitchen herbs.

Harvest time is a period of richness and plenty. It behooves the monk to pay close attention to the immutable rhythms of nature's clock, telling him to set aside other occupations for later and concentrate on the laborious work of the harvest. Work in the flower gardens also continues during the autumn months, though less intensively than during the summer. October and early November is a good time to divide and transplant the perennials. There are also some plants that need extra care, such as tender plants that must be brought into the greenhouse so they can survive for another year.

The Liturgy, too, has its own rhythm of seasonal and festal celebrations that, in our northern hemisphere, are closely connected with autumn and the harvest. On September 14 we celebrate in the monastery the feast of the Triumph of Christ's Glorious Cross. On that day the winter monastic schedule begins, which includes the monastic fast that, except for Sundays and feast days, lasts until Easter. During this time monks keep the ancient tradition of cutting down on the amount of food consumed, a practice which becomes a bit more severe during Advent and Lent. Fasting is not viewed negatively by monks, but more as a means to achieve a change of heart and bring the weakness of our nature under control. Monastic fasting tries to bring into balance the spiritual order and the natural order in the monk.

On November 1 we celebrate the solemnity of All Saints. This is a family feast, for the saints are God's friends and our intercessors. The saints are very real to monks, as we are profoundly rooted in the faith of the early undivided Church. At the beginning of our monastic life, each one of us receives a monastic name of a saint, who then becomes a model, friend, and protector. We monks believe that the saints in their home above never cease to intercede for us and to help us do our tasks on earth adequately and promptly. The communion of saints is a mystery that is indeed very real, very personal, and very comforting to the monk's heart. Deep inside we know that we are really never alone, for the Lord is there for us, the Mother of God is there for us, and our friends the saints are also there making strong pleading for us.

On November 11, monasteries celebrate the feast of St. Martin of Tours, an early monk and bishop who spent his life evangelizing France. It is an intimate monastic feast, for St. Martin, especially in France, is very much loved by monks and nuns. After the feast of St. Martin, we move on to the annual celebration of Thanksgiving, when we make a point of setting aside a day to bless the Lord and show him our gratitude for the miracle of a good harvest. Thanksgiving provides us the occasion to thank God not only for the harvest but also for all the blessings throughout the year. With Thanksgiving Day we reach the peak of the season of plenty and fruitfulness. After that the evenings begin to shorten in quite a dramatic way, and one senses the steady decline of autumn as it seeks to merge with the hastily arriving winter.

In the monastery autumn stands apart. It is a season that allows us to see our lives reflected in the beauty of the land all around us. As the trees let go of the glory of their leaves, however, so too are we called to let go of our encumbrances and press ahead with our spiritual striving. And as we let go of all that is superfluous and unwarranted in our monastic lives, we receive from the Lord the gift of inner peace and the promise of eternal life.

> May He support us all the day long,
> Till the shades lengthen
> And the evening comes,
> And the busy world is hushed,
> And the fever of life is over,
> And our work is done.
> Then in His mercy . . .
> May He give us a safe lodging,
> And a holy rest,
> And peace at the last.
> JOHN HENRY CARDINAL NEWMAN

Glossary:
A Monastic Vocabulary

ABBACY: the term of tenure of an abbot or abbess.

ABBATIAL CHURCH: the monastic church of an abbey.

ABBESS: the mother and leader of a monastery of nuns.

ABBEY: a monastery ruled by an abbot or abbess.

ABBOT: the father and leader of a monastery of monks.

ABSTINENCE: an ancient ascetic monastic practice in which monks and nuns abstain from eating meat.

ACCEDIA: a state of despondency and lethargy, a distaste developed by the monk for his spiritual or monastic life.

ADVENT: the liturgical season that precedes and prepares for Christmas.

ANGELUS: a monastic devotion honoring the mystery of the Incarnation which is announced by a bell in the morning, at noon, and in the evening.

ANTIPHON: a short text taken from the Psalms and usually sung before and after the psalm.

ANTIPHONALE: a book that contains the music (chant) and text for the hours of the Divine Office.

APATHEIA: a Greek term used by the desert fathers to indicate a state of being no longer controlled or motivated by passions.

APOTHEGM: a short saying given by a desert father or mother to a disciple; a sentence that is life-giving and full of wisdom.

ARCHIVIST: the monk or nun in charge of the monastery archives.

ASCETIC: a person engaged in a life of asceticism.

ASCETICISM: the practice of self-discipline and self-denial.

ASPERGES: The ritual of sprinkling holy water on monks or nuns at the end of Compline before they retire for the night. It is also done on Sundays at the beginning of the conventual Mass.

"BENEDICAMUS DOMINO": a monastic greeting between monks and also to those who arrive at a monastery.

BENEDICITE: The blessing asked before a meal and at other occasions.

BOW: A deep inclination of the body used frequently by monks as a sign of reverence and respect.

BREVIARY: The books that contain all the parts of the Divine Office.

CANTORS: The monks in charge of intoning or singing alone parts of the Mass and the Office such as antiphons, hymns, responses, etc.

CELL: The monastic room or bedroom where the monk lives alone with God.

CELLARER: The name given to the bursar of the monastery. He is also in charge of coordinating the work in the monastery.

CENOBITES: Monks who live in a community.

CENOBIUM: The original word for monastery.

CHAPTER: The body of monks, similar to a board, who meet at required times under the direction of the abbot or prior to discuss important matters concerning the life of the monastery.

CHAPTER-ROOM: The room in the monastery where the monastic chapter is held.

CHOIR: The part of the monastic church where monks or nuns participate in the Eucharist and sing the hours of the Office.

CLAPPERS: Wooden instruments used to call the monastic community to services on the last days of Holy Week. Used instead of a bell.

CLOISTER: An enclosed section of the monastic building often used for processions.

COLLATIO: The small evening meal taken on fast days.

COMPLINE: The night prayer of the monk; the last hour of the Office.

CONVERSATIO: One of the vows made by the monk during his monastic profession by which he commits himself to follow the monastic way of life.

COWL: The choir habit of the monks used for liturgical functions and ceremonies. It is worn on top of the regular habit.

DESERT: The birthplace of monasticism and its constant ideal.

DESERT FATHERS AND MOTHERS: The Spirit-filled initiators of the monastic movement.

DISCRETION: The teaching of St. Benedict that counsels the monk to practice moderation and balance in all things. A characteristic monastic virtue.

DIVINE OFFICE: The traditional term for the monastic liturgy of the hours. It comprises: Vigils, Lauds, Prime, Terce, Sext, None, Vespers, and Compline, and it is sung at certain precise times of the day.

DORMITORY: A section of the monastic building that contains the cells of the monks.

DOXOLOGY: A short prayer of praise to the Holy Trinity sung habitually at the end of the Psalms and the hymn.

ELDER: Name given to senior monks who are usually well versed and experienced in the ways of the spiritual life.

ENCLOSURE: The private section of the monastery reserved for the monks and nuns to foster an atmosphere of silence and prayer.

EREMITICAL: Elements pertaining to the life of hermits or solitary monks.

EUCHARIST: The celebration of the Lord's Supper. Also called the Liturgy of the Mass.

GARDENER: The monk or nun in charge of the monastery gardens.

GRADUALE: The book that contains the chants for the proper and the Ordinary of the Mass.

GREAT SILENCE: The time of strict silence at night between the Office of Compline and the end of Lauds.

GREGORIAN CHANT: The monodic and rhythmically free Latin chant used habitually in the monastic liturgical services. The Chant has also been adapted to the English language by some monasteries.

GUESTHOUSE: The portion of the monastic buildings assigned to outside guests.

GUEST MASTER: The monk assigned to the care of monastery guests.

HABIT: The monastic garb or clothing of monks and nuns.

HEBDOMADARIAN: The monk or nun appointed to lead the Offices of the week.

HERMIT: A monk who lives in solitude.

HERMITESS: A nun who lives in solitude.

HESYCHIA: Stillness, quiet, repose, tranquillity. The inner state of constant prayer and union with God. It is the ideal of every monk and nun.

HOLY WATER: Blessed water used daily as part of monastic ritual.

HORARION: The daily schedule of the monastery.

HOUR: Name given to individual parts of the Divine Office.

HUMILITY: A virtue particularly stressed by all the fathers and mothers of monasticism.

HYMN: A song of praise to God used at the beginning of each hour of the Divine Office.

ICONOGRAPHER: The monk or nun who has the task and gift of painting icons in the monastery.

ICONS: Holy images or representations of the Lord, the Mother of God, and the saints used in the monastery's worship or in the private devotions of monks and nuns.

INFIRMARIAN: The monk assigned with the care of the sick in a monastery.

INSTRUMENTS OF GOOD WORKS: Monastic counsels given in chapter 4 of the Rule of St. Benedict.

INTROIT: Entrance antiphon taken from the Proper of the Mass and sung at the beginning of the Eucharistic celebration.

INVESTITURE: The monastic ritual in which the novice receives the monastic habit.

INVITATORY: The psalm (usually 94) and antiphon sung at the beginning of the Office of Vigils.

KALENDAS, KALENDARIUM: The listing by month and date of liturgical feasts.

KYRIE ELEISON: A petition prayer meaning "Lord, have mercy" used in parts of the Mass and at the conclusion of all the Offices. This short Greek prayer is one of the most ancient Christian prayers, which the early monks used as a method of achieving continual prayer.

LAUDS: The second Office of the day, which is sung at dawn. It is also sometimes called Morning Praise, for the psalms used in this hour are usually all psalms of praise.

LECTIO DIVINA: A monastic practice of "reading the things of God," especially of the Bible, where God through the sacred text speaks directly to the monk's heart.

LENT: The forty days of fasting and penitential practice that precedes the solemn celebration of Holy Week and Easter.

LESSONS: Readings taken from the scriptures and from the fathers read during liturgical celebrations.

LIBRARY: The special room in the monastery that contains all its books.

"LISTEN": The first word of the *Rule of St. Benedict.*

LITURGY: The formal worship of the monastic community, which comprises the celebration of the Eucharist and the Divine Office.

LUCERNARIUM: Part of the Office of Vespers in which the first evening lights are lighted. It consists of Psalm 140, the prayers of the light, and the Hymn of Light. It is one of the most ancient parts of the Office, which the early church inherited from the synagogue. It commemorates the evening sacrifice of Christ.

MAGNIFICAT: The Canticle of Mary, sung every evening at Vespers.

MARTYROLOGY: The book that contains the sum of the liturgical feasts and the commemoration of the saints of each day. It is read daily to announce the feast or commemorations for the following day.

MATINS: The night Office or Office of readings, which today goes by an earlier name: the Office of Vigils.

METANOIA: Repentance, conversion, change of heart.

MISSAL: The altar book containing all the parts pertaining to the Roman Mass.

MONASTERY: The dwelling place for persons who embrace the monastic life.

MONASTIC: All elements pertaining to the life of monks or nuns.

MONASTIC DECORUM: The personal etiquette, manners, or form of conduct appropriate for monks and nuns.

MONASTIC FAST: The period of fasting which monks and nuns undertake annually that encompasses September 14 till Easter, except for Sundays and feast days.

MONASTIC PROFESSION: The rite by which the monk or nun engages himself or herself permanently to the monastic state of life.

MONASTICISM: The establishment or state of life of monks and nuns.

MONK: Comes from *Monos,* which means alone, single, solitary.

NONE: The ninth hour of the Office, sung around 3 P.M.

NOVICE: Candidate for the monastic life who is being trained to become a monk.

NOVICE MASTER: The senior monk in charge of training the novices or new candidates to the monastic life.

NOVITIATE: The period of time a monk spends in formal training.

NUN: A woman who professes monastic life.

OBEDIENCE: One of the three monastic vows by which the monk renounces his own will and agrees to live under the direction of a Rule.

OBLATE: A person who is affiliated to a particular monastery and has a spiritual link to it.

OBSERVANCE: The particular practices of a monastery in following the Rule or ancient customs.

OCTAVE: The eight-day period following the celebration for a Solemnity or major feast.

OFFICE: See "DIVINE OFFICE."

ONOMASTIC: The feast day of the saint for whom a monk or nun is named.

OPUS DEI: It means "Work of God" and it is applied by St. Benedict exclusively to the liturgical hours of the Divine Office.

OPUS MANUUM: Expression used by St. Benedict referring to the manual work of monks.

ORATORY: The word used by St. Benedict to describe the place where monks pray and chant the *Opus Dei.*

ORDINARY: The unchanging parts of the Mass and Office which are repeated at each of their respective celebrations.

PARLOR: The room or rooms in the monastery used to receive and speak to outside visitors.

PAX: Peace. The motto and ideal of monasteries that live under the Rule of St. Benedict.

PORTER: The monk posted at the entrance of the monastery to greet visitors.

POSTULANT: A newly arrived candidate to the monastic life.

PRAYER OF THE HEART: Expression used to refer to inner prayer and more specifically to the recitation of the Jesus' prayer.

PRIME: The first of the Little Hours of the Opus Dei, usually sung around 6 A.M. (It has been suppressed in the Roman Office and consequently many monasteries omit it today in their daily observance.)

PRIOR: The second in command after the abbot. Also, the superior in monasteries where there are no abbots.

PRIORY: A monastery directed by a prior instead of an abbot.

PROCESSION: Liturgical ritual used frequently in monasteries.

PROFESSION: *See* "MONASTIC PROFESSION."

PROPER: The particular parts of the Mass or Office which change in consonance with the season or feast being celebrated.

PROSTRATION: A symbolic form of penance or ritual of prayer used by monks which comes from the early desert tradition.

PSALMODY: The daily singing of the Psalms in the Divine Office, which has its origins in synagogue worship and that of the early church.

PSALTER: The book of Psalms used daily in the Divine Office.

QUIES: Rest. Quiet. Stillness. The state of repose the soul enjoys when it is united with God.

REFECTORIAN: The monk in charge of the refectory.

REFECTORY: The dining hall of the monastery where the monks partake of their daily meals.

REPENTANCE: Inner sorrow for sin. Deep desire for conversion.

RESPONSORY: The response sung during the Office after a lesson from the scripture or a reading from the fathers. It is usually taken from the Psalms.

RITUALE: The book containing all the established ceremonies of a monastery.

RULE: From the Latin Regula, it is the book that is the basis and guide for the life of monks and nuns. A Rule contains both the spirit and the prescribed legislation for monastic life.

SACRISTAN: The monk assigned to the care of the sacristy, vestments, and sacred vessels of the altar.

SACRISTY: A room attached to the monastic church where all the utensils connected with the celebration of the liturgy are kept.

SANDALS: Shoes consisting of soles strapped to the feet and usually worn by monks and nuns following ancient monastic practice.

SCAPULAR: A part of the monastic habit worn over the tunic which hangs almost to the floor. It originated from the work apron used by monks.

SEQUENCE: A poetic hymn sung on special feasts during Mass before the Allelluia.

SEXT: The sixth hour of the Divine Office, usually said at noon.

SILENCE: A constant monastic practice that encourages in the monk the spirit of recollection and continual union with God.

SIMPLICITY: A gospel virtue that encourages in the monk a state of being simple, innocent, and uncompounded. It frees the monk from false pretense and worldly cares.

SOLITUDE: The physical space where the monk or nun retreats from the noise of the world to seek God in quiet and seclusion.

SPIRITUAL FATHER OR MOTHER: The monk or nun experienced in the spiritual life that serves as mentor to beginners and those less experienced.

STABILITY: The monastic vow binding the monk or nun to a particular monastery and community.

STATIO: The monastic practice of assembling in silence for a few minutes in the Cloister outside the church before processing inside for the celebration of Mass or the Office. It is a practice that fosters recollection as a preparation for prayer.

TERCE: The Hour of the Office sung at the third hour of the day, around 9 A.M.

THEOTOKOS: Greek word given to the Virgin Mary that means Mother of God.

TRADITION: In monastic life it means the handing down of teachings, beliefs, customs, and practices from one generation of monks to another.

TUNIC: A simple slip-on garment, belted at the waist, which is the main component of the monastic habit.

VERSICLE: A brief response sung during the Divine Office.

VESPERS: The evening hour of the Divine Office sung at sunset—when the first lamps were lighted in antiquity.

VIGILS: *See* "MATINS."

VOW: A promise made to God.

VOX DEI: It means voice of God, and it is an expression given by monks to the ringing and sounds of bells which call them at appointed times to the worship of God.

WEEKLY READER: The monk or nun who is appointed to do the reading during the coming week in the refectory.

Selected Bibliography

St. Athanasius. *The Life of St. Antony*. Baltimore: Newman Press, 1978.

Burton-Christie, Douglas. *The Word in the Desert*. New York: Oxford University Press, 1993.

Cassian, St. John. *Conferences*. New York: Paulist Press, 1985.

Climacus, St. John. *The Ladder of Divine Ascent*. New York: Paulist Press, 1982.

Cummings, Charles. *Monastic Practices*. Kalamazoo: Cistercian Publications, 1986.

De Vogue, Dom Adalbert. *The Rule of St. Benedict. A Doctrinal and Spiritual Commentary*. Kalamazoo: Cistercian Publications, 1983.

Evdokimov, Paul. *The Struggle with God*. New York: Paulist Press, 1966.

Hourlier, Dom Jacques. *Reflections on the Spirituality of Gregorian Chant*. Orleans: Paraclete Press, 1995.

Leclercq, Dom Jean. *The Love of Learning and the Desire for God*. New York: Fordham University Press, 1960.

Levi, Peter. *The Frontiers of Paradise*. London: Collins, 1987.

Louf, Dom Andre. *The Cistercian Way*. Kalamazoo: Cistercian Publications, 1983.

Maria, Mother. *Sceptum Regale*. Library of Orthodox Thinking, 1973.

Merton, Thomas. *Contemplative Prayer*. Herder and Herder, 1969.

———. *The Monastic Journey*. New York: Doubleday, 1978.

———. *The Silent Life*. New York: Farrar, Straus & Cudahy 1957.

———. *Thoughts in Solitude*. New York: Farrar, Straus & Cudahy, 1958.

The New Jerusalem Bible. New York: Doubleday, 1985.

The Rule of St. Benedict. Translated, with Introduction and Notes. A.C. Meisel and M.L. del Mastro. New York: Doubleday, 1975.

The Rule of St. Benedict. In Latin and English with Notes. Ed. Timothy Fry. Collegeville: Liturgical Press, 1981.

Thekla, Sister. *Mother Maria: Her Life in Letters.* New York: Paulist Press, 1979.

Van Zeller, Dom Herbert. *The Holy Rule.* New York: Sheed and Ward, 1958.

Waddell, Helen. *The Desert Fathers.* Ann Arbor: University of Michigan Press, 1957.

Ward, Sr. Benedicta. *Harlots of the Desert.* Kalamazoo: Cistercian Publications, 1987.

———. *The Sayings of the Desert Fathers.* Kalamazoo: Cistercian Publications, 1975.